To my diaper-free family:
David, Kaiva, Isadora, and Cooper.

TABLE OF CONTENTS

WELCOME! 1

   WELCOME TO THE GO DIAPER FREE BOOK 2
   WHO I AM 4
   WHO THIS BOOK IS FOR 7
   WHY I WROTE THIS BOOK BACKWARD 8
   SPECIAL READERS' AREA ACCESS 11
   HOW THIS BOOK IS DIFFERENT 12

CHAPTER 1: HOW TO EC 13

   THE NUTSHELL VERSION 14
      Parts 1 and 2... A pretty simple overview 14
      The Basics, Part 1: When does baby need to potty? 15
      The Basics, Part 2: How to potty your baby 16
   WHAT TO KNOW BEFORE BEGINNING 19
      What is EC? 19
      The Forms You'll Need 20
      A Big Picture Message 20
   THE BASICS, PART 1: WHEN DOES BABY NEED TO POTTY? 22
      Breakdown of Part 1, Step 1: Observe 24
      Breakdown of Part 1, Step 2: Cue 29
         Common Cues 30
      Breakdown of Part 1, Step 3: Notice Baby's Signals 31
         Types of Baby Signals 35
         Babywearing Signals 37
      Breakdown of Part 1, Step 4: Notice Baby's Natural Timing 38
      Breakdown of Part 1, Step 5: Become Aware of Generic Timing 40
         Generic Timing: Common Times that Babies Need to Go 42
      Breakdown of Part 1, Step 6: Notice Your Intuition 44
   THE BASICS, PART 2: HOW TO POTTY YOUR BABY 47
      Breakdown of Part 2, Step 1: Notice It's Potty Time 48
      Breakdown of Part 2, Step 2: Acknowledge, Undress, & Go to
      Potty Space 51
         Possible Potty Environments 53
         Possible Potty Receptacles 53
      Breakdown of Part 2, Step 3: Position & Cue 55
      Breakdown of Part 2, Step 4: Be Patient 57
      Breakdown of Part 2, Step 5: Notice When Baby Says "I'm Finished" 61
      Breakdown of Part 2, Step 6: Reflect or Say Nothing 63
      Breakdown of Part 2, Step 7: Clean Up 67

MOBILE BABY + YOUNG TODDLER MODIFICATIONS AND MAINTENANCE 71
The Optional Hybrid Plan for 12-18 months 71
Diapers or not?.. 72
Misses 72
Signals/Prompting/Cueing... 72
Troubleshooting 73
Maintenance Tips for Mobile Babies.. 73
The Re-set 75
33 tips for starting older (all ages between 6-18 months)........................ 76
POSITIONS GALLERY 83
The Positions & Other Photos 84
Indoor Pottying Positions 86
Outdoor Pottying Positions 114
Car Pottying Positions 126
Setting Up a Soaker Pad on Any Surface... 140
Breastfeeding Pottying Positions 145
Aiming the Boy Pottying Positions 148
Other Position Photos 156

CHAPTER 2: UNIQUE SITUATIONS + HOW-TO'S 167

7 UNIQUE SITUATIONS 168
Pottying While Breastfeeding 169
Pottying in Nature... 171
City Pottying.. 174
Car Pottying (next to parked car)... 175
Car Pottying (inside parked car)... 176
Cold Weather ECing 178
Travel and EC 179
NIGHTTIME EC.. 185
Introduction 186
Key Points + How-to's 187
Night Pottying Troubleshooting.. 195
PART-TIME EC.. 205
EC for Working Parents (& Other Part-timers)... 206
DIAPERS + DIAPER-FREE TIME... 213
Introduction 214
How to Diaper with EC... 215
Do I Have to Do Away with Diapers? 232
Doing Regular Diaper-free Time, Responsibly... 235
THE BUILDING BLOCKS OF POTTY INDEPENDENCE 241
Steps to Potty Independence + Graduation 242
The Building Blocks: What Can Be Taught, and When.............................. 247
When Full-on Completion is Possible 252
How to Complete the EC Process 253

WHO I AM

I'm Andrea. I'm 37 years old (now), a mother of (now) 3, and in between even more loads of laundry and cooking meals, I've managed to write a few books on Elimination Communication.

Before having a baby, I earned my Master's in Psychology and practiced for many years. I thought I had a pretty good handle on child psychology until I became a mom...and that's when the real learning began. With my homebirth and subsequent years of actual mothering, I've certainly earned a residual PhD.

I am the Director of DiaperFreeBaby, Inc.. Their organization has certainly influenced my personal EC practice from the beginning and I continue to seek their support. They fully endorse the work I've done to continue EC's forward movement and I am honored to serve as their Director and continue to make free EC support groups available to people worldwide.

I am also the Director of the new Go Diaper Free Certified Consultant Training Program and am enlisting parents from all over the globe to help teach and support EC in their local communities.

So, that's about it for my relevant credentials. Now about me and EC and this book...

I have been doing Elimination Communication with my babies since the day each was born. We caught the first tarry poo in the potty, and I have been hooked on avoiding poopy diapers ever since.

4

WELCOME!

I heard about EC in 2006 when the first of my friends-of-friends had a child. Someone said, "Yeah, they don't use diapers! They do this thing where you communicate with your baby instead. She pees in the sink!"

I was intrigued. I thought to myself, *When I have my first child, I'm going to do that.*

When I became pregnant in 2009, I knew beyond a shadow of a doubt that I wanted to do what tribal folks all over the world do: natural pottying.

However, the information available at the time seemed overwhelming, complex, and inaccessible for me at that "placenta-brain" phase of pre- and post-partum. I read the relevant sections again and again, and still lacked confidence.

All I wanted was a clear step-by-step of how to start EC at birth.

So, after a few months of working it out as I went, I decided to create my first book to help other parents learn how to begin EC with any age baby...presented in a simplified format.

It's been such an enriching journey that in the future I plan to begin filming a comparative documentary on pottying around the world. I am curious to know the intimate details of pottying across the Earth's tribal communities.

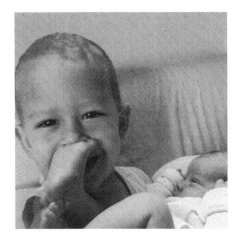

Well, enough about me...you certainly didn't buy this book solely to learn about me and my sweet little journey. Let's get on with the show!

Warmly,

Andrea

PS - I wrote this book in a conversational format, so please pardon any occasional frankness, tartness, enthusiasm, dry humor, or anything else that might not seem up to professional par. This was a conscious choice to make reading (and learning) a little bit more fun and personal. Oh, and sometimes I repeat myself, which I do intentionally to reinforce important stuff. :)

WHO THIS BOOK IS FOR

This book is for anyone with a young baby who is yearning for a natural alternative to full-time diapering and conventional toilet training.

This book is for pregnant mamas and their partners who want to give their babies the utmost in natural, responsive, and gentle parenting, from the get-go...but don't have the brainwaves or energy available to read complex instructions or heavy books.

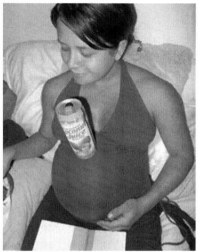

(like I was)

This book is also for folks who want to have a baby someday in the future and are researching different parenting tools.

The earlier parents start EC, the smoother the journey. I recommend beginning at the first optimum window, 0-4 months, but if you've arrived here and you're beyond that window (and within the first 12 months), you'll be just fine. I have special instructions for you.

If you've got a baby who's 12 months +, don't you leave yet! You can apply the principles within this book to your early start at conventional toilet training, too.

WHY I WROTE THIS BOOK BACKWARD...

Many books are written in this order: first some history, then the underlying philosophy, and finally what the book promised to cover...at the end. Well, mine wasn't. I've written my book backward!

I've a good reason for this: If you never reach the part of this book that's about how to do EC, you may never do it.

I know how it is to be expecting a little one. The pregnant woman's brain dims to just a flicker of what it used to be. Calculators and thesauruses become desperately necessary, yet difficult to use.

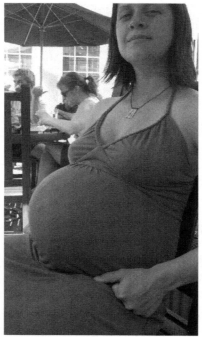

(me again)

Movement...slows...way...down.

WELCOME!

Partners of pregnant women are equally "not all there." They're either worried about what's coming next; busy preparing and providing for what's coming next; terrified and avoiding all thoughts of what's coming next; so excited about what's coming next that they can't focus.

So, for those expecting parents who are walking through jello, I put the juice first.

For those of you who already have a young baby or newborn (and perhaps other older children), need I even write how much you've got going on? Hence, juice first.

When I was pregnant, I wanted the juice first. With pictures and pretty drawings and flow charts. I went into ECing knowing it's what I wanted to do, and I didn't need the history til much later (when my body and brain recovered). 8 months later!

Perhaps you're the same. If you're not, no worries, go to the Table of Contents and read the Background & Philosophy section first...have it any way you like.

But if you need to get to the point as much as I did, I wrote this book backward for you. You're welcome.

Now let's get started...from the end...

...because every serene moment counts....

SPECIAL READERS' AREA ACCESS

Throughout this book I mention the Private Support Group, Video Library, extra Troubleshooting Knowledge Base, and Downloadable Forms. If you'd like to access all of this extra information, visit godiaperfree.com/upgrade and follow the instructions.

HOW THIS BOOK IS DIFFERENT

(from my previous works)

Those of you who've heard of my first book, *EC Simplified: Infant Potty Training Made Easy*, and my second book, *Go Diaper Free: A simple guide to elimination communication, versions 1-4*, might be wondering how this book is different.

In this 5th Anniversary Edition, I've decided to go back to my roots. EC Simplified was originally only available in ebook format. It also didn't cover a lot of the findings we've discovered through the *act* of doing EC, as a community, over the past 5 years. Go Diaper Free was written to improve upon EC Simplified, and was broken up into 3 age ranges for simplicity's sake.

However, when the paperback was introduced in 2015, it was just plain too big and cumbersome to be "simple."

So, in this Anniversary Edition, I've lumped everything back into one primary instruction, and added notes for mobile babies and young toddlers (6-18 months) in supplement to the primary instructions. I feel this honors the simplicity of what EC truly is. I've also made the 12-18 month old alternate instructions (the hybrid plan) a separate download, available in the Book Owners' website, to keep this book 100% pure EC.

This Anniversary Edition also contains the improvements included in Go Diaper Free versions 1-4, such as The Nutshell Version, the alternative instructions for young toddlers (which is more of an EC/potty training hybrid), a new positions gallery, a new online Book Owners' Website, and a bunch of little details like how to prevent teaching your baby to pee on the floor (um, very important).

I think you will find that this Anniversary Edition is **the new conclusive guide** to starting, maintaining, troubleshooting, and wrapping up an EC practice with a 0-18 month old baby.

And that, my friends, is how this book is different from my other two.

Shall we begin?

CHAPTER 1: HOW TO EC

THE NUTSHELL VERSION

In this section we'll start out with the nutshell version of how to start EC, a simple definition, and some basic keys to keep in mind while beginning, just so you have your feet immediately under you.

As you embark on this exciting journey, continue with the rest of this book's sections to learn more about starting EC (in more detail), mobile baby and young toddler considerations, positions, back-up diapering, philosophy, and anything else you might need to know to get started.

Remember that you do NOT have to do EC full-time, but some sort of consistency is a great idea. There's a section on Part-time EC that I hope you'll read. Okay…now for the nutshell of what in the world you'll be learning.

PARTS 1 AND 2… A PRETTY SIMPLE OVERVIEW

I've divided the whole process of starting EC into two basic parts:

- Part 1: How to know when your baby needs to potty
- Part 2: How to potty your baby

Depending on your baby's age, this basic process will vary ever so slightly. You'll see that when you get to the notes on mobile babies and young toddlers. So here's the general Nutshell Version *first* so you can understand the big picture….

THE BASICS, PART 1: WHEN DOES BABY NEED TO POTTY?

No matter the age of your child, you will follow this basic pattern to learn *when* your baby needs you to help her go potty.

Please note that you won't take your child to the potty for the hours or days you're doing Part 1...you're in learning and observation mode, so you'll just do that until you decide to start Part 2.

This is the *very rough* version, in words:

You'll observe your child during naked time (or modify it with a sumo-style diaper) for a few hours or days (however long it takes), and during this time, every time you see her pee or poo you'll either cue along with her, or if she's a bit older and more developed you'll go ahead and say a word that you'd eventually like for her to say to you when she needs to go. This is called sound association.

During this observation time, you'll also note your baby's signals, aka peepee dance (this is what happens right before she goes). You may find nothing. No worries.

You'll also note her natural timing, or how long she normally takes to go pee or poo after feeding or waking. Meanwhile, you'll also be studying up on what times most babies need to pee (or when it's really convenient or sensible for you to offer). Incorporate these, however you wish, into your daily routines. You'll also check in with your own intuition during observation time...which you may notice during this "getting to know you" part of The Basics.

That's what you're lookin' for, in an over-simplified nutshell.

Here's something for those of you who are more visual learners:

15

The nutshell of part 1

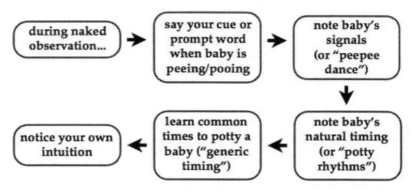

THE BASICS, PART 2: HOW TO POTTY YOUR BABY

Once you learn all that, you STOP Part 1. Here is the nutshell of Part 2.

It's time to begin actually pottying your child. Like this:

You'll notice one of the four things that you learned during Part 1 (a signal from him, his natural timing is nigh, it's a common time to potty the babe, or your intuition kicks you).

You'll either state (not ASK...you'll rarely ask if they need to go) it's potty time or just stay silent and let your actions speak for you.

Whether your child can walk or not dictates how you get to the potty space, but know that you somehow get there and get the pants and/or diaper back-up out of the way (undress).

Then you either get your wee baby into position or have your young toddler sit down and cue – or say your prompt word – during the pee or poo. Once. Then wait. {sounds of pee or poo going into the proper container}

Once done, which should be pretty obvious, you simply clean up and re-dress your babe and you're all finished. Oh, and if you are inclined to reflect what she did (you went pee) then go right ahead. If not, saying less also shows confidence, so you may do that.

Here's a visual of that process I just described:

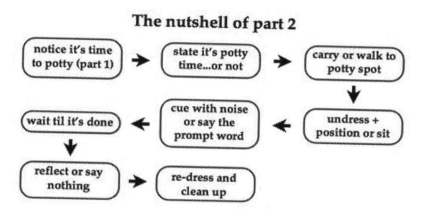

And that, my friends, is the very, very, very simplified nutshell of pottying your baby. PLEASE don't skip the details for starting EC in the next section. Thanks!

Oh yes...and as your baby gets older, things will change. You'll hand off the baton and teach certain parts, making her feel like an important part of the process (she is!). And you'll become involved less and less. But (roughly) for months 0-16, you can pretty much expect to be doing the bulk of the pottying work, be it prompting, cueing, holding, directing, or teaching.

It's Time to Learn How to Do
EC with Your Baby

The next two sections are the most important parts of this book: The Basics Part 1 & 2.

Read Part 1 to learn *When Does Baby Need To Potty?* This involves learning signals, timing, and cues for a few days or weeks.

Then, read Part 2 for *How To Potty Your Baby*...it's time to begin pottying.

As you embark on this exciting journey, equipped with The Basics, continue with the remainder of this book to learn more about positions, back-up diapering, wrapping up the process, philosophy, gear, and support.

WHAT TO KNOW BEFORE BEGINNING

WHAT IS EC?

EC is a non-coercive, gentle way to potty an infant from as early as birth, following a baby's natural awareness of her elimination and her instincts to keep herself, her caregivers, and her sleep space dry.

A FEW KEYS

- EC is gentle. Hold your baby gently, speak gently, and handle the whole process with care.
- EC is non-coercive. It doesn't involve praise, rewards, punishment, force, anger, or consequences.
- EC is about communication, connection, responsive caregiving, and making future potty independence smoother and less confusing. It is not about goals, pressure, timelines, conventional "potty training," or completion (though I will show you how to complete should you want that).
- EC is not about hovering or obsessing. It's not about making your baby the center of your attention. It is about "keeping an ear out" (while you do grown-up things, perhaps while wearing your baby), and maintaining an awareness around & assisting with elimination (as we do when we notice that the baby needs to eat or sleep). The cause of 95% of potty pauses is offering too much and/or hovering!
- EC is fun. Laugh often. Marvel in the awesomeness of what you're witnessing (the easy times and the more challenging times).
- If you find yourself becoming frustrated about or stressed out by ECing, take a breath, regain your center, let a few misses happen, refrain from punishing or complaining to the baby, and seek support (hop on to the Private Support Group right away!). Don't quit...just zoom out and re-collect yourself for a little bit. I KNOW it can be challenging. We are here to support you, as anyone who does EC needs support.

THE FORMS YOU'LL NEED

To find all the forms, signs, and guides I've made for you to help you on your journey, gain access at godiaperfree.com/upgrade and visit the Downloads section. Then download and print as you need them. You do *not* have to use these forms, but if you're a forms type of person, they're there to help you.

A BIG PICTURE MESSAGE

There are a few things parents and caregivers should know prior to beginning the journey to potty independence, infant or young toddler:

- Your child follows your lead. If you, the parent, are equipped, you both will do much, much better at this. (In other words, read up and get support!)
- You are not going to psychologically damage your child to potty teach before 2 years old. So long as you don't tie them to the potty chair, you can not possibly damage them for life.
- Your child does have sphincter control (as early as day one) and can indeed use those muscles.

- Being gentle sometimes includes being firm. You may have to [gently] put your foot down, at times that make sense to you, occasionally in the process. Children thrive on boundaries, including babies, and especially including toddlers.
- Mastery is good for your child. Especially toddlers. You are not rushing anything by teaching tools for independence in this personal process.
- Long-term, repetitive tasks can not be consistently held in the brain until its development finishes up between 14-18 months. Have age-appropriate expectations. Basically: before this brain development is finished (marked by the ability to sing a song or do a certain process the same every single time), you are going to need to help your child in some way, and it may be in a different way each time until he gets it consistently on his own.
- When doing EC, you will have to pass the baton. You can't hold children over a potty forever and then one day expect them to go on their own. Passing the baton = teaching stuff so they can be independent. We will cover that in depth, so don't worry!
- You might never, ever stop prompting (well, maybe when your baby becomes a teenager). This is part of the process. Potty independence is a team effort. Just like reminding your child to eat when it's time, you will occasionally have to notice that 'peepee dance' and prompt your child to go.
- The learning curve is completely non-linear. Stick with it and eventually you'll end up with a straight line. Things come together in a random, unpredictable order. Rely on noticing the tiny successes to keep you motivated.
- Notice when you're obsessing or hovering in this process, and try to stop. Your child will react negatively to this unseen pressure. If your child becomes resistant, teach something, give more independence, wrap it up completely, or back off some. Offer less often. But stay with it. Tricky balance, I know!

Now it's time to learn EC!

THE BASICS, PART 1:
WHEN DOES BABY NEED TO POTTY?

Here's an overview of how you'll learn when your baby needs to go and how to cue along with him, with more details on the following pages.

> **During this learning stage, *do not* take your baby to the potty just yet.** Your goal is to Observe, Notice, Learn, & Build Association around **Signals, Timing, Cues, & Intuition.**

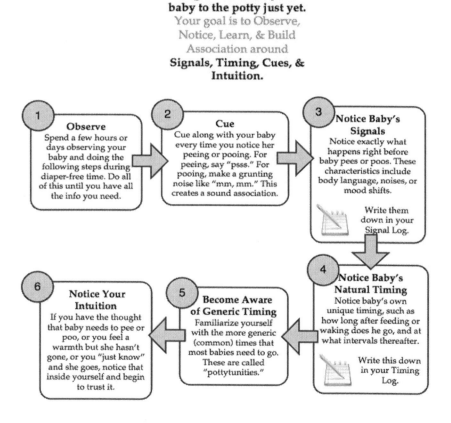

1 Observe
Spend a few hours or days observing your baby and doing the following steps during diaper-free time. Do all of this until you have all the info you need.

2 Cue
Cue along with your baby every time you notice her peeing or pooing. For peeing, say "psss." For pooing, make a grunting noise like "mm, mm." This creates a sound association.

3 Notice Baby's Signals
Notice exactly what happens right before baby pees or poos. These characteristics include body language, noises, or mood shifts.
Write them down in your Signal Log.

4 Notice Baby's Natural Timing
Notice baby's own unique timing, such as how long after feeding or waking does he go, and at what intervals thereafter.
Write this down in your Timing Log.

5 Become Aware of Generic Timing
Familiarize yourself with the more generic (common) times that most babies need to go. These are called "pottytunities."

6 Notice Your Intuition
If you have the thought that baby needs to pee or poo, or you feel a warmth but she hasn't gone, or you "just know" and she goes, notice that inside yourself and begin to trust it.

A TIP FROM ANDREA

Do all of the steps for Part 1 for several days or weeks **before** attempting to take baby to potty (we did it for the first 2 weeks after birth when I was in bed recovering anyway).

Benefits:
- baby will get used to the sound of your Cues and associate them with pottying
- you will get used to baby's Signals
- you will get used to baby's Natural Timing
- you will have time to learn Generic (Common) Timing
- you will give yourself some time to begin having Intuitions
- it will be less frustrating if you learn the Cues, Signals, and Timing first
- you will feel less pressure to do it "right."

If you feel you've gotten the hang of it after a shorter period of time & want to dive right in to Potty Time, feel free to go directly to Part 2.

Andrea

BREAKDOWN OF PART 1, STEP 1: OBSERVE

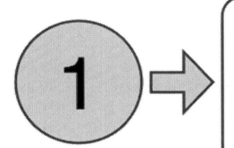

Observe
Spend a few hours or days observing your baby and doing the following steps during diaper-free time. Do all of this until you have all the info you need.

HOW TO DO NAKED DIAPER-FREE OBSERVATION TIME

You will do the following Steps 2-6 of Part 1 <u>during</u> diaper-free observation time. Here's how:

1. Observe your baby diaper-free in a warm, safe space (either on a bed, floor, or laying on your body or lap).
2. Use one or more layers of these under your baby to absorb the pee/poo* (this layering is known as a "soaker pad"):
   - a cloth prefold (which is just an absorbent cloth diaper)
   - a blanket (perhaps a cotton receiving blanket)
   - a 100% wool puddle pad (must have a blanket or prefold over it to absorb the pee)
   - a towel
   - a waterproof pad (has a cloth layer and a plastic layer)
   - a disposable incontinence pad, aka "Chucks Pad" (a common homebirth supply found at the drugstore)

example 1: Place your baby on a prefold over a towel over a waterproof pad over the sheets of your bed.

example 2: Place your baby on a prefold over a wool puddle pad on your lap.

example 3: While laying down, place your baby on a single cotton prefold over your naked belly/chest.

24

3. For boys who pee straight out/up, you can place a prefold over his penis and pay attention to when it gets wet. However, if you can brave a few messy pees without a covering, you'll get <u>much</u> more information.
4. For older babies, observe on a non-carpeted floor, or outdoors, where messes can be easily cleaned.
5. After you've gathered your info (1-2 days), discontinue **naked** time unless your child, for some strange reason, doesn't pee on the floor.

example 4: Line your living room in yoga mats, towels, whatever, and have the mini potty nearby, in the room with you.

example 5: Observe outdoors or over any non-carpeted floor.

example 6: With a mobile or walking baby, use a sumo-style diaper (see How to Diaper with EC) with a burp cloth (which is much thinner than a cloth diaper insert) and diaper belt, and check occasionally for wetness, recording your findings later on in this process.

6. For mobile or walking babies, while you are doing observation, when your baby begins to pee or poo, have the potty nearby and bring the baby to the potty every time, for consistency. Gently say "wait" or "potty" when he begins to go on the ground, then transport him to the proper receptacle (or bring the receptacle to him). Or just let him experiment…your choice! See what works for you. We will cover this more later.

If you are uncomfortable doing or unable to do naked diaper-free observation time, simply use a back-up (undies, trainers, or try diapering Sumo-style – see How to Diaper with EC) and try to notice when it gets wet. Or, focus more on cueing with in-diaper poos and using timing as a tool (next pages).

*For a step-by-step photo demonstration of how to set up your soaker pad for diaper-free observation, see the Positions section.

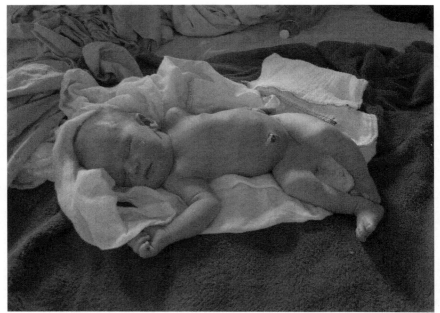

Our early diaper-free time consisted of a few pre-folds, a soft blanket, and a towel.

WHEN TO DO DIAPER-FREE OBSERVATION TIME

1. Frequently during the newborn weeks when you're mostly skin-to-skin anyway (prime observation time!)
2. At a designated time each day in an "okay" area for regular diaper-free time (if pee-on-floor is a problem, use clothing)
3. Before bath time (for easy cleanup)
4. For an older baby, outside on a nice sunny day (with sunscreen if he needs it). Have the potty nearby and bring the baby to the potty *even when outdoors*, for consistency. Remember to say "wait" or "potty" when he begins to go on the ground, then transport him to the proper receptacle. Or just let him experiment…your choice! See what works for you.
5. Any time you need to re-discover your baby's signals, natural timing, or both.

WHY DIAPER-FREE TIME IS IMPORTANT

You have to learn some things to do EC effectively. Having your babe naked or diaper-free will help you gather this information in an efficient manner. Although you should stop naked observation if/when you've gathered all your info (even if that info says "there is no signal"), here's why it's important to have regular, responsible* diaper-free time throughout your baby's life:

1. Baby will experience "cause & effect." In other words, *my bladder fills, I release it, and this wet stuff comes out*. This tremendously increases the speed of learning.
2. Baby will have more mobility without the diaper on, which could increase motor skills and enable earlier self-dressing.
3. Time without a diaper is a great time to nurture baby's skin, giving it fresh air and sunlight, discouraging diaper rash.
4. Baby can explore her genital areas and develop a positive self-perception around sexuality, cleanliness, and her body image.

27

5. Parents will learn more about the baby's signals and natural timing by observing while diaper-free. In fact, trying to learn these things with a diaper on is nearly impossible.

*AN IMPORTANT NOTE: HOW TO MAINTAIN RESPONSIBLE DIAPER-FREE TIME AFTER OBSERVATION ENDS?

"Diaper-free" means free from exclusive dependence upon diapers. It doesn't mean having a naked kiddo running around peeing all over your floor 24/7. You should model the "right" thing.

This has become a major issue for the majority of ECers. Let's prevent that by reading the section called Doing Regular Diaper-free Time, Responsibly, shall we?

A FEW REMINDERS...

In the Beginning
In this beginning stage, do as much or as little diaper-free observation time as you are able and comfortable with…up until you've gathered the necessary information, that is. Again, you'll do Steps 2-6 (next pages) *during* this diaper-free observation time that you've just learned how to do here in Step 1. By collecting this info prior to pottying your baby, you'll have an advantage!

Ongoing Diaper-free Time
As your baby grows, offer diaper-free time as often as you wish, whether you're observing signals/timing or not, and be sure to avoid teaching him to pee on the floor by bringing the 9 month + baby to the potty when he begins to go, while saying "wait" or "potty." And use clothing, underwear, or trainers as a back-up to avoid teaching "pee wherever."

For more info on this and more about how or whether to continue diaper-free time after observation time has served its purpose, please see Doing Regular Diaper-free Time, Responsibly.

Now on to the next Step where you'll learn *what* you should do while doing naked diaper-free observation time!

On to Steps 2-6 where we learn <u>what to do</u> while observing. →

28

BREAKDOWN OF PART 1, STEP 2: CUE

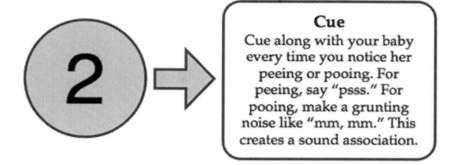

> ## Cue
> Cue along with your baby every time you notice her peeing or pooing. For peeing, say "psss." For pooing, make a grunting noise like "mm, mm." This creates a sound association.

HOW TO MAKE A SOUND ASSOCIATION (CUE)

While you are observing your baby during diaper-free time (Step 1), every time you notice pee or poo coming out, make your chosen Cue.

This helps establish sound association with your baby, and eventually the Cue will become his prompt to release and go potty. The more you do this when you see him go, the more he will associate going to the bathroom with your noise.

CUEING IN A DIAPER

Sometimes you get the chance to practice cueing when your baby isn't diaper-free!

For instance, if your baby's in a diaper and you notice she's going, Cue along with her anyway, as if she were naked. If you can also get her into Position while Cueing…even better. This builds association & familiarity with both.

It's obviously much easier to notice & Cue along with a baby who's pooing – the grimaced face, staring, grunting, or squirming (or by hearing it coming out) is a straight giveaway.

Which Cue Do You Want to Use?

Choose any noise of your choice to tell your baby that you see him peeing or pooing.

Common Cues

- for pee, the noise of running water: "psss" or "ssss"
- for poo, grunting: "mm, mm" or "ugh, ugh"
- clicking
- blowing air on baby's head
- using the word "peepee" or "poopoo"
- using the sign language sign for "potty" or "toilet"
- just letting the position be the cue
- or alternating between a pee noise and a poo noise if baby's doing both.

Whichever you choose, be consistent. Over time, you may decide to change cues depending on how your baby responds as he grows.

When Cueing Must Turn Into Something Else

If it doesn't feel "right" to make a "psss" or grunting noise while your baby is peeing or pooing, or if it seems like she's at the age where using a *word* association might make more sense than using a *sound* association (usually at around 8-9 months), you might want to cue with a word instead of a noise, as suggested above...or perhaps a word and a sign. This is where the "cue" becomes language...and eventually your baby will begin to use this word or sign as her signal to you!

30

BREAKDOWN OF PART 1, STEP 3: NOTICE BABY'S SIGNALS

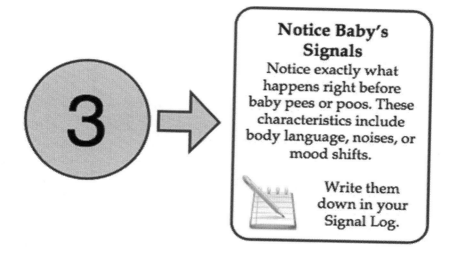

As you get used to seeing your baby eliminate and cueing along with her, the next step is to notice <u>exactly</u> what happens <u>right before</u> the pee or poo.

Write this down in your **Baby's Signal Log** (available in the Book Owners' Area) or make note of it in your mind. Sometimes identifying your baby's signals is quite natural...you notice or sense a "shift" in the baby's state (body language, noises, mood) and then, voila!... she pees. Her signals may be very obvious.

Sometimes you may know the signal but the time lapse between signal and pee/poo is so tiny that you think, "How will I ever catch anything?" No worries. Over time, these time lapses will become longer and longer as the muscles become stronger and the mind develops the proper pottying associations (your consistency, cues, and positioning all contribute to this flow).

Signals are usually easier to identify with pre-poo versus pre-pee. Go ahead and gaze at your little cutie during diaper-free observation and pay attention to the subtle and not-so-subtle signals that may appear.

IF YOUR BABY DOESN'T SIGNAL

Sometimes babies' signals are super-subtle, or may seem non-existent. You may look and look and find nothing.

- Try again *after* turning off your phone, Facebook, & computer.
- Those who don't signal clearly at first may start signaling when they get older...or vice versa.
- It's sometimes easier to pick up on signals with your 2nd baby than your first (if you did EC with the 1st).
- Most babies signal very clearly when in a sling/carrier...try it!
- Sometimes you may need to check in over many days to catch the signals. Be patient, open your head, heart, and soul to listening on all the possible levels, and see what happens.
- Some babies will <u>only</u> signal when they have a diaper <u>on</u>. How to test it out? Spend some time with your baby in a prefold without a cover, or Sumo-style (see How to Diaper with EC). Notice what happens right before she soaks it.

If this doesn't work, your baby just plain doesn't signal (or you just plain don't see it because it's so darn subtle), so rely on timing (natural and generic) and intuition (next pages)...the other 3 Roads to Potty Time. They work great...no worries! See Troubleshooting for more details.

A PROGRESSION OF MY FIRST BABY'S SIGNALS

Here's a sampling of my first baby's signals over the months. Your baby's signals can and will vary.

Newborn

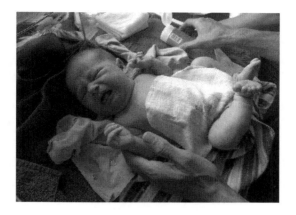

- crying, fussiness, wriggling in bed, movement after stillness, grimacing & grunting for poo

Mobile (for him, 5 months)

my grimace poo face

wriggling/ crawling during sleep

- all of what we had for Newborn Signals (crying, fussiness, wriggling in bed, movement after stillness, grimacing & grunting for poo) plus crawling to us in bed or on the floor while fussing, wriggling/ crawling during sleep, flipping head side to side during sleep, standing up or jumping in carrier

Very Mobile, Standing, First Steps (for him, starting at 7-10 months)

banging on the toilet

34

crawling to mom and grimacing

- crawling to bathroom or shower (sometimes coming back & signaling to us with a look or sound, then crawling to the bathroom again), standing at & banging on the door to be let outside to pee, banging on toilet, crawling to us and standing up at the back of our legs while 'talking' and then crying, saying "wee-wee," signing by waving his hands, going to a particular 'poo place' (to get into a good stand/ squat position to push it out) while looking at us and grimacing/ grunting, playing with penis (especially with an erection), squatting and getting very silent, blowing raspberries, getting very agitated or hyper (especially when wearing a diaper), jumping in carrier or while standing, crying out suddenly and loudly, picking up mini potty and looking at us, grabbing at or trying to remove his diaper or underwear

TYPES OF BABY SIGNALS

Different ways babies tell us they need to pee or poo:
- sudden or increased fussiness
- cry or scream
- shift from stillness to movement
- shift from movement to stillness
- squirming or wriggling (especially in bed if co-sleeping)

- for older ages during sleep, crying out, crawling in bed, talking, or flipping head from side to side
- grimace or other concentrated poo face (may look like a smile)
- popping off the breast while feeding; difficulty latching
- grunting or bearing down (may also be done squatting/standing)
- staring off into the distance
- trembling, shaking, hiccuping, yawning, rubbing face or nose, shivering
- heavier breathing
- "peenie-weenie" – a partial erection that means baby boy needs to go
- grabbing at genitals, especially if squatting or looking at you or the bathroom
- blowing raspberries (trying to imitate your Cue)
- passing gas (may indicate pee, poo, or both)
- looking at...pointing at...or crawling to ==> you, the potty, or the bathroom
- arching back in or trying to stand in arms (or in carrier...see below)
- "phantom pee" (feels warm but baby hasn't peed)
- trying to "escape" the high chair, car seat, your lap, or the baby carrier (by standing, arching, etc.)
- trying to remove diaper or grabbing at diaper or underwear
- sudden agitation or hyperactivity

Babywearing Signals

- sudden crying or fussiness
- wriggling
- feet pushing against you
- trying to stand up in the carrier
- bouncing
- arching out of the carrier
- "phantom pee" on either side (feels warm but baby hasn't peed)

BREAKDOWN OF PART 1, STEP 4: NOTICE BABY'S NATURAL TIMING

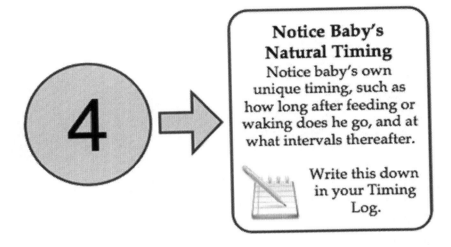

Notice Baby's Natural Timing
Notice baby's own unique timing, such as how long after feeding or waking does he go, and at what intervals thereafter.

Write this down in your Timing Log.

To simplify this step, while observing your baby, keep an eye on the clock and **see how many minutes it takes for baby to pee or poo after these 2 events only, in this order**:

- after feeding
- after waking

…and how much time passes after that til the next pee/poo, and the next, and the next (called "intervals").

HOW TO RECORD BABY'S TIMING

Grab a watch, a pencil, and download & print your Baby's Natural Timing Log (available in the Book Owners' Area). Start by timing pees & poos after feeding, recording the intervals in your Log. Then, time pee/poo intervals after baby *wakes* from sleep. I've made one Log where you can chart feeding & waking on the same sheet, and two other Logs if you want to separate the two on different sheets. Use whichever forms work for you or simply make note of the timing in your mind. Again, start with feeding to observe & record Natural Timing…it's easier to get the hang of.

38

At the very least, observe & record during the minimum of 1/2 hour per day of diaper-free observation time, starting with feeding, utilizing the Log. If you can, observe all day long for your baby's *overall patterns and rhythms*, always referring to the timing intervals as they follow eating and waking (ie: don't just start timing randomly!).

And while you do this, please pretend like you aren't...hovering and hyperfocusing are known causes of potty resistance.

The result of this observation and recording is your baby's Natural Timing. In other words, you will discover the natural rhythms of his digestive and elimination systems, which vary slightly from baby to baby.

Remember...every baby is different.
As his muscles develop and bladder grows, more time will span between his pees. **Baby's natural timing intervals will expand over time.** As he starts solid foods, his bowel movements may lessen (and harden tremendously). As time passes, your awareness of his inner clock will sharpen.

And as he learns that he can depend on you to (at least try to) help him potty, building mutual trust, he will begin to "hold" it and his natural timing will spread out a bit more.

In the beginning months, babies pee ALL the time (and boys do more than girls). It's wise to remember that the frequency *will* reduce soon.

BREAKDOWN OF PART 1, STEP 5: BECOME AWARE OF GENERIC TIMING

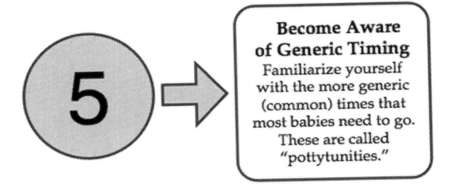

Become Aware of Generic Timing
Familiarize yourself with the more generic (common) times that most babies need to go. These are called "pottytunities."

WHAT IS GENERIC TIMING?

In addition to your baby's unique Natural Timing (her own elimination patterns), there's something called Generic Timing, or Transition Times.

Generic Timing just means that the majority of babies have to go at certain times throughout the day. This usually occurs before or after an event during which baby naturally holds it (like being in a sling, a carseat, in your arms, or asleep).* It also could be a time when you find it convenient to potty your child (like when you get to a store, or prior to gymnastics playtime). This is, more specifically, called a Transition Time.

In EC lingo, Generic Timing is fondly known as a "Pottytunity."

*Will my baby really hold it where he's supposed to? As babies get older some will have a miss in the carseat or high chair because they are used to "sitting" on the potty, and after a few minutes sitting there, it feels like time to release. Many babies, however, will never miss in these places because they associate the carseat or high chair with a place that's meant to stay unspoiled. *It just depends on the baby.*

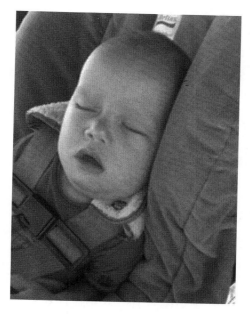

SO, WILL MY BABY PEE WHILE SHE'S IN MY ARMS?

If baby's in your arms, the majority of the time she will not pee on you. That said, ECers (including tribal mamas) all over the world sometimes get peed on while holding a baby. It happens when the signal is missed or ignored…or perhaps baby just doesn't give one at all. She might even be experimenting….

IF YOU <u>DO</u> GET PEED ON…

Calmly move the baby to the other side of your body without negatively reacting. You could choose to reflect, matter-of-factly, "You just peed on me," or say nothing. Remain calm, neutral, and unmoved. Making a big deal out of it will just upset the both of you. Learn what you can from what just happened.

Get to know these common times to offer a pottytunity. If you try at one of the times listed below, you are likely to make a catch (especially first thing in the morning!).

GENERIC TIMING: COMMON TIMES THAT BABIES NEED TO GO

- upon waking from sleep
- during a diaper change
- before or after a bath
- after a miss, as baby's bladder may not have fully emptied
- after taking baby out of anything she's been in for a while (carseat, stroller, baby carrier/sling, jumper, sitting aid toy, or high chair)
- before putting baby into anything she'll be in for a while (carseat, stroller, baby carrier/sling, jumper, sitting aid toy, or high chair)

OTHER POTTYTUNITIES (TRANSITION TIMES)

- offer potty before leaving anywhere
- offer potty upon arriving anywhere

Offer pottytunities...upon waking...

...when taking baby out of anything or before putting baby into anything

...and, before or after using a high chair.

BREAKDOWN OF PART 1, STEP 6: NOTICE YOUR INTUITION

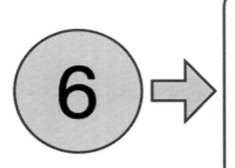

> **Notice Your Intuition**
> If you have the thought that baby needs to pee or poo, or you feel a warmth but she hasn't gone, or you "just know" and she goes, notice that inside yourself and begin to trust it.

WHAT IS INTUITION?

Sometimes you "just know."

Women in tribal societies are extremely in touch with their intuition. According to the EC texts I've read, indigenous women often potty their babies nonchalantly in mid-conversation or activity. They do it in a matter-of-fact way, often responding to what an outsider might think is "nothing."

That is intuition in action, and you may have it too! Some people are able to pick up on and act timely upon their intuitive hunches. Some simply aren't wired that way.

WHAT IT MIGHT BE LIKE...

Notice your thoughts and your misses and catches. See if the thoughts, feelings, hunches, sensations, and perhaps even visuals preceding the pee/poo correspond to your baby actually going. You might be more intuitive than you guessed.

Do you have a funny feeling that baby may need to go (or can't possibly need to go again)? Does the word "pee" or "poo" cross your mind? Are you imagining baby needing to pee? Do you suddenly have to pee yourself? Some people swear they smell pee or poo before it comes out; others have a vivid thought or insistence inside and are "sure" baby needs to go. I sometimes have dreams that the baby needs to pee, and wake up to find that he needs to go. **Notice your intuition and listen to it.**

IF YOU DON'T HAVE IT

Sadly, intuition in the Western world is a buried, lost art in many cases. But luckily, as a culture, we are rediscovering this inner guidance system and beginning to trust it once again.

If you don't feel or think any of the above intuitive thoughts or feelings, don't fret! Just rely on Signals and Timing and you'll be fine. Not everyone has potty intuition (sometimes it doesn't appear until the second baby!). You may or may not have it. It's all good, either way.

OLDER CHILDREN MIGHT

If you have other children, they tend to be hyper-intuitive. Listen to their intuitions as well and invite them to share a hunch that baby may need to potty.

ADVICE FROM A SAGE

This is from a woman on the EC Yahoo! Group:

"Always act on sudden random potty thoughts immediately (you are usually picking up on subconscious signals)."

CONGRATULATIONS!
YOU'VE FINISHED THE BASICS, PART 1.

Basically, you've learned that there are 4 roads that lead to pottying:

The 4 Roads to Potty Time

After several days or weeks of practicing Part 1 and recording your notes in the Logs, download this month's sign (available in the Book Owners' Area) and fill it out:

My Baby's EC This Month
(Signals & Timing fill-in-the-blank)
January-December

Hang it on your fridge to remind you (and your family) what your baby's patterns are this month, and do a new one every month thereafter, noting the inevitable changes.

NEXT UP: The Basics Part 2

THE BASICS, PART 2:
HOW TO POTTY YOUR BABY

Here's an overview of how to actually take your baby to the potty, start to finish, with more details on the following pages.

It's time to start pottying!

Your goal is to **practice responding** to the Signals, Timing, & Intuition you just learned about...you will begin to **Position & Cue** your baby and learn how to adjust your style & rhythm through experimentation *with* your baby.

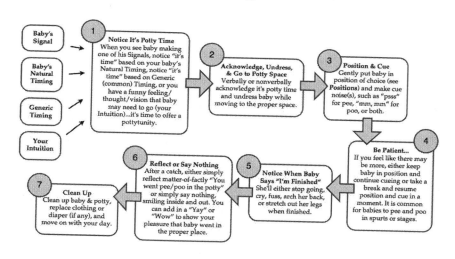

Baby's Signal

Baby's Natural Timing

Generic Timing

Your Intuition

1 — Notice It's Potty Time
When you see baby making one of his Signals, notice "it's time" based on your baby's Natural Timing, notice "it's time" based on Generic (common) Timing, or you have a funny feeling/thought/vision that baby may need to go (your Intuition)...it's time to offer a pottytunity.

2 — Acknowledge, Undress, & Go to Potty Space
Verbally or nonverbally acknowledge it's potty time and undress baby while moving to the proper space.

3 — Position & Cue
Gently put baby in position of choice (see Positions) and make cue noise(s), such as "psss" for pee, "mm, mm" for poo, or both.

4 — Be Patient...
If you feel like there may be more, either keep baby in position and continue cueing or take a break and resume position and cue in a moment. It is common for babies to pee and poo in spurts or stages.

5 — Notice When Baby Says "I'm Finished"
She'll either stop going, cry, fuss, arch her back, or stretch out her legs when finished.

6 — Reflect or Say Nothing
After a catch, either simply reflect matter-of-factly "You went pee/poo in the potty" or simply say nothing, smiling inside and out. You can add in a "Yay" or "Wow" to show your pleasure that baby went in the proper place.

7 — Clean Up
Clean up baby & potty, replace clothing or diaper (if any), and move on with your day.

BREAKDOWN OF PART 2, STEP 1: NOTICE IT'S POTTY TIME

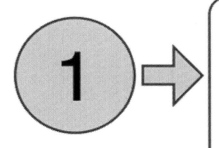

Notice It's Potty Time
When you see baby making one of his Signals, notice "it's time" based on your baby's Natural Timing, notice "it's time" based on Generic (common) Timing, or you have a funny feeling/thought/vision that baby may need to go (your Intuition)...it's time to offer a pottytunity.

HOW TO KNOW IT'S POTTY TIME

Now that you're in Part 2, the Potty Time arena, you can put into action what you learned and observed in Part 1. But how do you know when to potty? Well, the 4 events that you mastered in Part 1 may mean it's potty time…

1. Baby's SIGNAL
2. Baby's NATURAL TIMING
3. GENERIC TIMING or TRANSITION TIME
4. Your INTUITION

HOW ABOUT SOME ROLE-PLAY EVERYONE?

Here are 6 sample scenarios to help you see what leads to potty time. #1 is about Signaling, #2 about Natural Timing, #3 shows a combination of both Signaling and Natural Timing, #4 is about Generic Timing, #5 is about Intuition, and, finally, #6 illustrates a combination of Intuition and Natural Timing.

1. So you're sitting around and your baby is playing nicely, and all of a sudden she gets grumpy and starts crying. That's a **Signal** you've come to know and you see if she needs to potty.

2. Your baby is playing nicely after you fed her. It's been about 10 minutes and you know she usually needs to go by now. You offer her the chance to potty, knowing her usual **Natural Timing**.

3. You fed your baby 10 minutes ago and she is playing nicely until all of a sudden her energy shifts, she gets a bit grumpy, and she starts crying. You put the two together: (a) she just ate (**Natural Timing**), and (b) she is **Signaling** you. You offer her the potty.

4. You are about to transfer your baby from the baby carrier to the carseat after grocery shopping. You offer her a pottytunity first (based on **Generic Timing** or **Transition Times**). When you get home 15 minutes later, you offer another pottytunity upon getting her out of the carseat (also based on **Generic Timing** or **Transition Times**).

5. You are carrying your baby around the house without his diaper on, when all of a sudden you feel warm and wet…as if he's soaked you! You move him to the other hip and find yourself to be completely dry (this was a "phantom" pee…a.k.a. **Intuition**). You offer him a pottytunity and he goes!

49

6. You are cooking dinner and have the thought "the baby needs to pee" (**Intuition**). It's been about 20 minutes since she last breastfed, which is her usual time to potty (**Natural Timing**)…but the thought "the baby needs to pee" keeps nagging you (**Intuition**) til you decide to leave the stove and offer the baby a Pottytunity. Voila! She pees.

Remember: These 4 events may shift over time…with every miss and every catch, remain open to change & evolution.

BREAKDOWN OF PART 2, STEP 2: ACKNOWLEDGE, UNDRESS, & GO TO POTTY SPACE

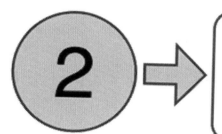

Acknowledge, Undress, & Go to Potty Space
Verbally or nonverbally acknowledge it's potty time and undress baby while moving to the proper space.

ACKNOWLEDGING IT'S TIME TO POTTY

There are several ways to acknowledge to your baby that it's time to potty, that you're working on taking her to the bathroom, and to just hang on a second and she'll experience the ultimate release and relief. Here are three:

1. Verbally: Note that we don't "ask" our babies if they need to pee. We simply make a statement, like: "I'm thinking you may need to pee. Let's go to the bathroom and see." "Let's go peepee!" "It's Peepee Time!!"

2. Nonverbally: Use sign language to communicate the question or expression. The most common sign for pottying is the ASL sign for "toilet" (it's the letter "T," shaking). To sign "toilet," make your hand into a fist with your thumb sticking out between your pointer and middle fingers, shaking side to side like this:

3. Mentally: Think a thought to yourself like: I'm going to take you to the bathroom now and see if you need to potty.

The mental way (#3) is what I assume to be the most common way people in tribal cultures acknowledge potty time. They generally don't make a big deal about it...they just have the thought, offer the potty, and move on with their day in a matter-of-fact way, usually without a word. It's likely unconscious.

In the US, we like to speak about most things with our children. Some use way more words than others. I don't think talking or being silent hurts, either way...it's up to you and your parenting style to decide how/if/when to acknowledge that it's potty time. Please just note that this acknowledgment is optional.

UNDRESS

This one's pretty straight-forward. Get whatever's in the way (if anything)...off of your baby. Diaper, pants, training pants, undies...get 'em off swiftly but gently. Check for wetness as you do this.*

You will learn the key to "dressing for success" with experience. There are ways to keep your baby warm, comfortable, and (if you prefer) contained (with a diaper or training pants)...WHILE still making it easy to potty him.

For more on what types of clothing work best with EC & where to get them, please see the Supply List. For more on diapering as a back-up, see the section called How to Diaper with EC.

*CHECK FOR WETNESS NOW...

If baby had on bottoms, check for wetness WHILE you undress him to see if you "missed" some or all of the pee.

Offer the potty anyway, even if the diaper is a little wet. Any wetness means he either "pre-peed" (a little trickle came out while he was trying to wait) or you missed the last pee and he was too busy to tell you, and now it's time for a second pee. However, if you notice baby protests against the next step (Position & Cue), AND his diaper feels wet, you might have missed the whole thing. Re-diaper and try again next time.

TAKE BABY TO POTTY SPACE

Where you take baby to pee/poo (Environment) and in what (Receptacle) is your choice. Some options for both are listed below.

It's not necessary to take baby to same space every time, especially in the early months. Please remember that your baby may change preferences over time, so keep a few creative ideas in your pocket about where to potty.

If you potty in a public space (indoors or out), try to find and use a public restroom. Using the classic EC hold over a public toilet or sink is an easy & sanitary method (so long as you clean the sink). If you must potty outside or in a mini potty somewhere, please be discreet and clean up after yourselves.

POSSIBLE POTTY *ENVIRONMENTS*

- bathroom (in toilet, mini potty, sink, shower, bathtub)
- on bed (in a receptacle, of course)
- in the living room (in a mini potty)
- outside/in nature (backyard, park, side of road)
- within the car or next to the car (in a top hat potty, bowl, etc, or on the concrete or grass next to a parked car)
- in a public bathroom (sink or toilet)
- side of bed (into a shallow receptacle)

POSSIBLE POTTY *RECEPTACLES*

(see the Supply List section for more info)
- grown-up toilet, held over it (with or without a mirror or sticker stuck to inside of lid)
- grown-up toilet with toilet seat reducer
- sink (bathroom or kitchen)
- bathtub (good for boys)
- stand-up shower (also good for boys)

- mini potty
- potty chair
- top hat potty
- disposable, cloth/plastic-lined, or wool puddle pad
- any bowl-like container that works for you (ie: mixing bowl, tupperware bowl, chamber pot, etc.)
- shallow container (such as a wide rectangular or circular basin with low edges) for use next to bed on floor
- water bottle or jar (boys)
- frisbee or whatever else is laying around in your car

..*our bathroom has an "open door" policy.*

BREAKDOWN OF PART 2, STEP 3: POSITION & CUE

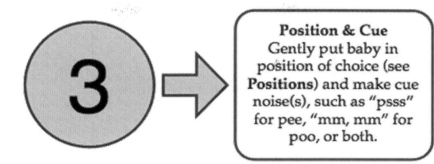

3

Position & Cue
Gently put baby in position of choice (see **Positions**) and make cue noise(s), such as "psss" for pee, "mm, mm" for poo, or both.

HOW TO POSITION & CUE

In Part 1, you practiced Sound Association to get your baby used to the Cue noise that you make while she goes.

In Part 2, this Cue now serves to remind her that it's okay to loosen those sphincters. It helps her practice releasing at will. With a little repetition, you'll get her used to associating both the Cue & the Position with the action of pottying, and she'll think: *"When I'm in this Position and I hear that Cue, it's cool to pee!"*

This is the "Classic EC hold."

So…put your baby in Position and make your Cue noise.
Tip: If you relax while you hold and cue your baby, she will relax and release more easily.

Gently hold your baby under the thighs, supporting his back and neck with your chest and belly.

For a photo gallery of various other positions & how to use them, please go to the Positions Gallery section.

IF YOU'RE TOO LATE, POSITION & CUE IN DIAPER

If for some reason you couldn't get his pants off in time, or you're not near an appropriate potty place/receptacle, simply position and cue *while your baby is wearing his diaper.*

This maintains the sound association. Some people talk to the baby about why he must go in his pants. "Sweetheart, there is nowhere I can potty you right now and I need you to pee in your diaper. I promise I will change it soon." Then change the diaper as soon as you are able.

Remember that your baby's preferred Position and Cue may shift over time. Your baby will communicate to you when he's ready for a change by arching his back, fussing, or not responding in the usual way. If you're pretty sure he needs to go, he may be giving you a sign that you need to get creative and evolve your strategies as his world expands.

Experiment with Position, Environment, Receptacle, and Cue noise. Whereas before you just needed to say "Psss" and he would instantly pee, now you may need to run the water, or take him to the big potty, sing a relaxing song, or just say, "PeePee."

Remember that sometimes he just doesn't need to go. Perhaps he's able to hold it longer now than before. Or, maybe he's experimenting with how long he can hold it and where he goes.

Just remember: Never <u>force</u> your baby to stay in a position that he's strongly resisting. Gently try something else (Position, Environment, Receptacle, Cue), run some water, sing a calming song, or wait til later when it's time again.

BREAKDOWN OF PART 2, STEP 4: BE PATIENT...

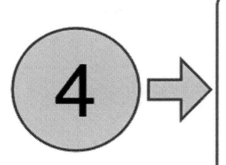

> **Be Patient...**
> If you feel like there may be more, either keep baby in position and continue cueing or take a break and resume position and cue in a moment. It is common for babies to pee and poo in spurts or stages.

PATIENCE WITH PEE

Pee can emerge in just one stream, one session...but when it "spurts" it comes out in a few sessions, with seconds or minutes between streams. It doesn't matter if the bladder's full...the baby will either release all of it at once or do it bit by bit.

Why? Well it could be on purpose, based on sensation, related to breathing, related to level of relaxation, or related to the amount of stimuli in the environment. It could also be the baby's personal "style."

From <u>one</u> full bladder, a baby may pee a bit now, more 2 minutes from now, and again 4 minutes from now. Take a deep breath. Note your baby's tendencies.

PATIENCE WITH POO

Pooing most commonly happens in stages. Obviously, every baby's different, but there are some reasons that stages occur.

When just breastfeeding, babies' poo is thin and runny. It can take several minutes to get it all out as the muscles inside aren't fully mature yet, and it takes some time for gravity to pitch in. And, pooping is a brand new thing for a brand new baby...it takes some getting used to.

After beginning solids, babies' poo becomes sausage-like and comes out like a Play-Doh Factory. Depending on your baby's system, it can still take a couple "sessions" to get it all out.

Pooing in Stages: If you're using the classic EC position (as drawn above), take the baby out of that position in between poos. This will allow the poo to flow down the colon and will give baby's thighs (and your muscles) a break.

You can hold her off to one side on one arm or find another good resting position that keeps the poo off of your shirt. If you've got a *younger baby* on a mini potty, simply be patient. Make eye contact, smile, ask her if she's got any more poo-poos.

If you know any infant massage techniques (such as gently "moving" the poo around the colon with a light stroke of the thumb from [looking at baby, facing each other] lower left up to upper left, then over to the upper right and down the right side), you can gently use them in between pushes.

In any case, toward what you believe is the end of the poo session ask, "Got any more poo-poos...or are you all finished?" If you are consistent with this latter part of the phrase, she will hear "are you all finished?" and realize that poo time is almost over and it's time to get all remaining poos out.

Over time, she may try to wrap it up with your communication.

Nothing happening...baby not relaxing? Take deep breaths with baby (to calm you both) or sing a potty song. Other parents like to engage their own stomach muscles while they grunt their cue...some believe when the baby feels it (as she's up against your stomach in the classic EC position) it helps her push and release.

MOBILE BABIES

Like I mentioned above, some older babies are so busy exploring that they only pause for a *brief moment* to push a little bit of poo out...and then they're off!

When baby is able to sit on the potty on her own, and crawl off on her own when she's finished with one push, empty the mini potty and keep an eye out for additional cues (squatting, grunting, looking at you) and put her back on the potty if she has another set of poo coming. (Again, keep that bathroom door shut if you've got one who might escape.)

I've done this up to four times in a row with a 9 month old! He crawled off in between each set and, a minute later, signaled again with a squat and grimace...then I'd sit him on the potty and he'd poo some more.

If you are able to engage her in some way or sing to her you may be able to catch her attention for the duration of a few poo-pushes on the potty. I like to sing "Twinkle, Twinkle" and do sign language with it. My boy became mesmerized for a good 2 pushes.

Otherwise, just be aware that there may be more later and hopefully your baby will signal again later...or perhaps you'll catch on to that "I need to poop again" body language.

MORNING PEES

If you breastfeed and co-sleep, chances are your baby's morning pees will come out in spurts that can be up to 5-10 minutes apart. Do a timing session and observe your baby in the morning, diaper-free. You may be surprised at how many sessions it takes for his bladder to empty!

And you might have assumed he just had to go like a racehorse in the mornings...that his bladder was full each time. But, alas, it was just that one full bladder, taking its time to leave.

MORNING POOS

Babies and adults emit a hormone while sleeping which keeps them from pooing in their sleep. Babies will generally need to poo first thing in the morning (especially at very young ages). Notice patterns with your younger baby and be patient while she gets that morning poo out in sleepy stages.

BREAKDOWN OF PART 2, STEP 5: NOTICE WHEN BABY SAYS "I'M FINISHED"

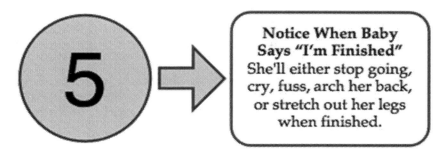

Notice When Baby Says "I'm Finished"
She'll either stop going, cry, fuss, arch her back, or stretch out her legs when finished.

HOW TO KNOW WHEN BABY'S FINISHED POTTYING

Your baby will tell you when he's finished pottying. Some "I'm finished" signs include:

- crying
- fussing
- stretching out legs
- arching back
- becoming active after being still
- stopping peeing and pooing (the very young baby may not signal that she is finished, other than stopping)
- falling asleep (especially newborns).

IF BABY DIDN'T GO, SAYS "I'M FINISHED," YOU STOP, AND THEN BABY GOES ON THE FLOOR 2 MINUTES LATER

Your baby may be experimenting with where and when she potties. She may be able to hold it longer than she used to.

She may not have liked the Environment, Position, Receptacle, or Cue you were using (even if she's liked it in the past). Perhaps if you try a different one next time, she won't just go on the floor after you take her off the potty.

Then again, she still might pee on the floor 2 minutes later. She might just be testing it out....

IF BABY IS SAYING "I'M FINISHED" BUT HASN'T POTTIED YET...AND YOU'RE PRETTY SURE HE HAS TO GO

If the timing tells you he should need to potty, or he is giving very clear signals, and yet he seems to be protesting by the above "I'm Finished" actions, this could mean you'll need to change it up a bit. Shift the scenery. Get creative.

Gently try something else (Position, Environment, Receptacle, Cue), run some water, or sing a calming song. Walk around for a little bit, relaxing yourself and pretending to just be walking, and then return to offer again.

If this doesn't work, simply wait until you receive another Signal or believe it may be Time again.

Remember: Never force your baby to stay in a position that he's resisting. Gently try something else (Position, Environment, Cue, Receptacle), run some water, sing a calming song, or wait til later when it's time again.

BREAKDOWN OF PART 2, STEP 6: REFLECT OR SAY NOTHING

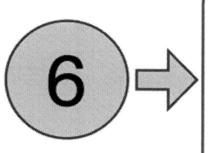

Reflect or Say Nothing
After a catch, either simply reflect matter-of-factly "You went pee/poo in the potty" or simply say nothing, smiling inside and out. You can add in a "Yay" or "Wow" to show your pleasure that baby went in the proper place.

WHAT TO SAY WHEN YOU CATCH A PEE/POO

Lots of people have differing opinions on this. Some people praise the baby, some people praise the action, others reflect what they see/saw, others state their pleasure, and still others choose to say nothing. After much research, experience, and thought, I recommend that you either (1) Reflect & Notice, or (2) Say Nothing. Before I get to those, here's a bit about why I no longer praise my baby.

WHY I NO LONGER PRAISE

After a catch, I used to praise and [albeit positively] judge. In the beginning, I would excitedly say, "Good peepee/poopoo!" and praise my baby for going. You can see proof of this in most of my videos which were taped before I had this epiphany.

After about 5 months, I reassessed this choice and decided to stop praising and start reflecting. Why? Well, I learned that as we praise children (for anything) they begin to do things to receive our praise and thus become extrinsically motivated. My hopes for my baby are the opposite: I want him to be motivated from within himself.

Further, when I would say that a peepee is "good," I implied that there is also a "bad" version out there. The child may think, *If I don't do it "right," am I "bad?"* This type of positive or negative language comes across as criticism, even if well-intentioned.

I don't think I did any permanent damage – my tone was appropriate. We all say "good job," right? It's okay every once in a while, I guess. But going to the bathroom is a natural process stemming from an inner motivation to take care of one's hygiene and is <u>not</u> meant to happen out of a motivation to please you.

1. Reflect & Notice

The alternative to praise is reflecting or noticing. This means describing what you see baby do without making a big deal out of it. You can even notice how *you* feel inside and express that. Some examples of how to notice and reflect are:

"You're peeing."
"You went pee/poo in the sink."
"You peed on the carpet. Peepee belongs in the bathroom."
"You pood in the potty. I'm excited...that's where poo goes."
"You feel relief because you peepeed."
"What a relief to pee. It feels good to pee outside of your diaper."
"You went poopoo....Ahhhh" (the noise "Ahhh" reflects the feeling of release)
"I feel so happy when you pee in the potty."

"Look at you peeing on the grass!"
"Look at [Baby's] poopoo in the potty!"
"I like that you pood in your potty."

Even words as simple as "Yay!" or "Wow!" will communicate the joy you feel when she pees in the desired place.

2. Say Nothing

In tribal cultures, most parents don't say anything upon a successful potty. It's expected that the baby should ask to go pee and the parent should take her (or that an unspoken intuition should guide it all). It's not really an exciting event because it is so socially ingrained as part of the "norm"...and thus there's never a big deal made of pottying. It's a natural given.

Some tribal parents do become upset about a miss in the middle of the kitchen, after the baby is old enough to "know better," but never do they become upset *with* the child, nor make her feel wrong...they are only displeased with the activity. This displeasure *clearly & honestly* demonstrates to the child which behaviors are acceptable and which are not.

WHICH WAY IS "CORRECT?"

Simply weigh whether you want to raise your child to be intrinsically (reflect or say nothing) or extrinsically (praise) motivated. Many of us have been conditioned to say it, so if "good job" slips out it probably won't obliterate baby's internal desire to do what's socially expected. But avoid "good boy" or "good girl."

WHAT YOU COULD SAY AFTER A MISS

If you've had a miss (ie: baby peed before you could offer her the potty), acknowledge that by saying something like, "You peepeed in your pants. Let me know next time and I will help you put it in the potty."

Be easy on yourself. It's not the end of the world if you have a miss. You want to model the kind of self-love that your baby will have, right? Be nice to Mom/Dad.

Ask yourself, "Now what did Mommy/Daddy learn from that?" **The best information is gathered by a miss!**

WHAT YOU COULD SAY AFTER A MIS-GUESS

If you have mis-guessed his need to potty (ie: he didn't have to go after all), acknowledge that gently. You can say to your baby, "Oh, you don't need to go peepee after all. Okay."

Never feel like you have to apologize...you didn't do anything wrong by offering. So long as you are gentle, open, and non-coercive, you are trying your best.

Next, ask yourself, "Now what did Mommy/Daddy learn from that?" **Great information can be gathered from a mis-guess!**

GRATITUDE AFTER A CATCH

After a smooth interaction (baby signals, I offer potty, he pees) I often say, "Thank you for letting Mama know you had to go pee." If it feels right for you to do that, gratitude is an awesome thing to model for your children.

BREAKDOWN OF PART 2, STEP 7: CLEAN UP

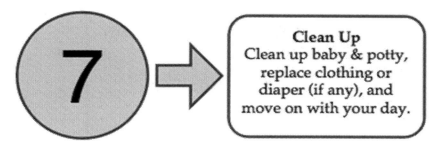

Clean Up
Clean up baby & potty, replace clothing or diaper (if any), and move on with your day.

HOW TO CLEAN UP

Clean-up is generally easier than changing a diaper (especially versus cleaning feces off of your baby's skin)...

Baby
- If a pee, blot (do not wipe hard) with a towel if you want to (pee is sterile).
- If a poo and you are near a sink, rinse baby's bum by scooping warm water onto it with your hand & towel blot dry.
- Alternatively, use wipes (disposable or water-moistened cloth wipe) but dry the skin afterward by blotting with a soft cloth (dry skin helps prevent diaper rash).
- Sometimes no wipe or splash is necessary, even if there was a poo (if it was swift and clean).

Potty
- Dump; (if a poo) rinse with soap and water; wipe or air-dry.
- Periodically sanitize with a sanitizing wipe or spray.

A FEW CLEAN-UP TIPS

- Breastfed babies' poo is typically runny and easily rinses down the sink (if you don't mind).
- If you use the sink or a mini-potty, always use a little water to rinse it and periodically wipe with a nontoxic antibacterial wipe (or use a spray and wipe).

- Some babies relax (and potty more easily) with the sound of the water running…you can warm up the water while she potties and help her relax at the same time…so when she's finished her bum gets rinsed with nice, warm water.
- For nighttime pottying, some folks leave a rag, small towel, or cloth diaper in the mini potty or bowl that soaks up the pee each time…this will help you avoid late-night spills and make clean-up easier.
- Instead of wiping a newborn baby's sensitive skin with a rag, toilet paper, or paper towel, gently blot with a soft cloth wipe.
- If you are outdoors and have discreetly pottied your baby, the pee will evaporate. However, to dispose of poo: if it's runny breastmilk poo, place earth matter (sand, soil, leaves, grass) on top of it; if it's solid, pick up the poo in a bag, tie it in a knot, and place it in a trash can. Make it a habit to carry biodegradable dog poo bags with you, such as BioBags, just for this use.

CONGRATULATIONS!
YOU'VE FINISHED LEARNING THE BASICS, PARTS 1 AND 2.

Remember…EC is about two-way communication. Your baby is teaching you yet another language of his, and you are learning how to engage with your with baby in this way. The goal is not perfection…**just keep focusing on listening & remaining curious to see what works best for both of you.**

Stay committed and confident. Seek help in the Private Support Group (gain access at godiaperfree.com/upgrade) for anything you've got a question about. Yay – I'm excited for you!

What's Next?
Next we'll review some Mobile Baby and Young Toddler Modifications and Maintenance Tips. If your baby is 6-18 months old, please read this section.

In the Book Owners' Website you'll find an Optional Hybrid Plan for 12-18 month Young Toddlers in case you want to do an EC/potty training blend. If you choose to download the Hybrid Plan, go ahead and review it and then go back and review the Modifications and Maintenance once more.

Then, we will wrap up the How to EC chapter with the Positions Gallery.

Then Chapter 2 covers Unique Situations + How-to's, including 7 unique situations plus nighttime EC, part-time EC, diapers and diaper-free time, and the building blocks of potty independence (or how to wrap things up).

After that is Chapter 3, the Philosophy and background part of the book, followed by Chapter 4, Troubleshooting. In the appendices you'll find the Supply List, Readers' Website information, resource and reference lists, and more of Andrea's work.

MOBILE BABY + YOUNG TODDLER MODIFICATIONS AND MAINTENANCE

In versions 1-4 of this book I broke down Parts 1 and 2 into age groups. For simplicity's sake, in this book I've combined them all into the previous two sections and included notes for mobile babies in those sections. However, for mobile babies and young toddlers there are some additional modifications and maintenance tips that I'd now like to mention.

If your baby is *not* yet mobile (ie: crawling, cruising, walking), skip this section and simply use the instructions in the previous two sections (The Basics Part 1 and Part 2). When baby becomes mobile you may wish to revisit this section at that time, or read it now to get a preview of what's to come.

If your baby IS mobile (is crawling, cruising, walking), welcome to the right place!

THE OPTIONAL HYBRID PLAN FOR 12-18 MONTHS

And, if your baby is 12-18 months and you believe a modified *potty training experience* might be more fitting (in other words, your baby is super-advanced and you'd like a much quicker wrap-up to EC, but you don't want to do a 3-day potty training bootcamp), please visit the Book Owners' Website to download the Hybrid Plan for Young Toddlers (access it at godiaperfree.com/upgrade). It is a mix of EC and my non-coercive potty training method described in my other book on potty training.

Otherwise, to stick to pure EC, go ahead and do Parts 1 and 2 (the previous two sections in this book), and then add in the following modifications and maintenance plans for your 6-18 month baby, wrapping it up with the section in this book called The Building Blocks of Potty Independence.

71

DIAPERS OR NOT?

If your baby is 6-9 months and not yet walking, you might want to wait until she starts walking to ditch the diapers completely. Meanwhile, dress her in a cloth diaper back-up or whatever helps her signal best until you feel it's time to quit the dipes. See When to Ditch the Diapers for more info.

If your baby is 9+ months and walking, after you get comfortable doing EC together you may choose to put him in underwear during the day and use a cloth diaper back-up at night if you choose (many do).

You may also choose to skip the training pants altogether – they are often too similar to diapers. Definitely skip the PullUps - they *are* diapers!

MISSES

If/when a miss happens, patiently and briefly say "Pee goes in the potty. Let me know and I can help you."

SIGNALS/PROMPTING/CUEING

When you notice a signal or see that it's time by noticing his peepee dance, begin integrating self-awareness reflections: "You're doing __x__ which means you need to pee/poop" and then transport your child to the potty while saying "potty." Transporting at this point can mean shuffling along together or actually picking him up.

You can also just say a word like "potty," "peepee," "I need to peepee," etc., when it's time to go, or when your child has begun to go. This word or phrase is essentially what you want him to start saying *to you* when he needs to pee. It will become HIS signal in the future. You no longer cue at this age with a "psss" or grunt noise.

Remember that you will still have to do regular prompting until the whole process is complete...and sometimes that can range from 14-20+ months depending on how you close up shop and how quickly that long term brain memory develops.

TROUBLESHOOTING

If things get unmanageable (ie: this whole things stresses you or hubby out beyond measure), use a cloth diaper back-up during the day for 1-2 weeks to ease into the practice with a diaper back-up as we do with younger babies.

If that doesn't do it for ya, and your baby's not getting it, you'll want to do a "re-set," then start over again. More on that in a sec....

But, most importantly, during maintenance mode, being in underwear will be pertinent. It is the most clear, confident sign you can give your child that things have changed...for good.

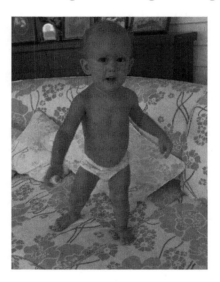

MAINTENANCE TIPS FOR MOBILE BABIES

You will keep ECing, part-time or full-time, as per everything in the previous Basics Part 1 and Part 2 sections and the rest of this book, but with these older, more-mobile-baby modifications:

1. Continue to do diaper-free time (ie: time without the diaper as a back-up, for instance, with undies, or just pants, or naked [if he doesn't just pee wherever], or split crotch...whatever you wish) at least 30 min-2 hrs per day.

2. Work on using the words "wait" and "potty" or "pee in potty" every time he starts to go on the floor or in his pants....whether diapered or not. Or say "I need to pee, Mama/Papa" to replace the "pee in potty" phrase. This will teach him what to say *to you* when he needs to go.

3. Continue making it fun to learn how to sit, and stay, on the potty. Modeling by the parents and other older kids (or youtube) is advised. Use books and songs and also encourage the job to be done "so we can go out to the living room and do other, more interesting and fun things!" Matter. Of. Fact.

4. Notice his signals and either set him on the potty or prompt him to take himself...depending on what he seems capable of doing.

5. Whatever part he resists...try to figure out a way to create autonomy in that part of the process. Teach something!

6. Use Generic Timing and whatever Natural Timing (the latter you learned in diaper-free time, or could learn in more diaper-free time) to offer when you think he needs to go, or before an outing when YOU need him to go before you leave.

7. Like this: (Sitting him on the potty) "Okay...one last pee before we put your pants on and leave." (Non-emotionally)

8. If at all, begin to use diapers as a back-up less and less. Use them as a tool. As you get the hang of things together, wean yourself off the trainers and into undies and pants, or pants only.

9. Encourage him to continue to tell you he needs to go. If he doesn't and pees his pants instead, you can tell him "Tell Mama/Papa next time and I'll help you put your pee in the potty." Keep it brief.

10. Eventually, teach him how to push down his pants. This is where just dressing him in loose elastic pants with no undies might help.....this can happen when you see it fit (we did it at around 17.5 months). Start with "This is how you put your thumbs in your pants." Sit him down and pull his pants halfway off, encouraging him to push or pull them the rest of the way off. Or, have him "push" his pants down while standing.

11. When your child reaches 18-20 months and you (the parent) feel ready, order my other book on non-coercive potty training - godiaperfree.com/potty-training-book - and finish him up, or, you can continue doing traditional EC via these maintenance tips, trusting that things will wrap up if you stay consistent and give him all the tools he needs for self-mastery. Your choice.

12. Continue communicating without over-talking. Enjoy connecting with your child more than being potty-centered.

THE RE-SET

As mentioned above in maintenance, if you need to do a "re-set" and start over, here's how:

Use a cloth diaper FULL-TIME (daytime) for 2 weeks. Mark it on your calendar. ONLY potty him when he is REALLY insisting...signaling loudly! (This may look slightly different than before, or the same.)

Otherwise, change him when he's wet. Don't overtalk anything. Tell him at the beginning of each day "You are going to wear a diaper all day today because you are still learning. If you need to pee or poo, tell me or [caregiver's name] and we will take it off for you so you can put your pee in the potty." Otherwise, nada.

Ignore misses for these 2 weeks! I know it will be hard, but please do so. During a re-set, you will not offer the potty at night either unless urgently requested by your baby...and follow the above instructions as well. Enjoy your break!

AFTER the 2 week re-set, I recommend you do the 1-2 days of naked time as described in the Optional Hybrid Plan for 0-18 month toddlers (found on the Book Owner's Website). You will do so with a peripheral focus (not hyper-focused, focus on connection and play only) including the whole transport-to-potty-every-time bit. Read about this in that section as well to understand what I mean.

THEN…dress him consistently in underwear or pants-only all day every day (again, this is if baby is 9+ months and/or walking). And do the maintenance mode I've described above. Continue to be peripheral about pottying. Remove it from the center of concerns. Remember that hyper-focus is the number one cause for potty pauses.

And that's it for the additional Mobile Baby and Young Toddler - specific instructions! As I said, this is a work in progress…so for any real-time updates to this method: visit our Private Support Group (gain access at godiaperfree.com/upgrade).

33 TIPS FOR STARTING OLDER (ALL AGES BETWEEN 6-18 MONTHS)

Prior to starting the creation of the working method for mobile babies and young toddlers (all in all, what I used to call Starting EC Older), I gathered 30+ tips for starting EC with an older, more mobile baby from various resources across the Internet and real life.

This is a collection of the most recent info…so please read through them and use what you like, discard what doesn't resonate. And…keep in mind that the most current info is in this whole section and in the Private Support Group…if the below 33 tips don't get you where you wanna go.

1. **Learn EC by following the EC instructions** in the corresponding section of this book, no matter what age your baby is: The Basics Parts 1 and 2.

2. **Decide whether you want to do EC part-time, occasionally, or full-time.** Do as much as you can without adding unnecessary stress to your lives. Remember that potty

learning at any age is inconvenient so it doesn't come as a surprise. See the section in this book called EC for Working Parents (& Other Part-timers) for more details on how to do EC part-time.

3. **Switch to cloth diapers or modified disposables immediately** (at least part-time) if you use disposables. See How to Diaper with EC for more info. You can eventually try switching to tiny trainers or undies if you wish. This change will provide you (& your baby) with information about when your baby is wet so you can change him immediately. It will also help you begin learning his patterns and signals.

4. **Change diapers immediately upon soiling.** Break the habit of letting your baby sit in wetness. Either time your diaper changes to happen more frequently or use a cloth diaper, held in place sumo-style, which will help you know immediately when baby is wet. See How to Diaper with EC.

5. **Do naked diaper-free time at times, and do it responsibly.** This allows your older, diaper-dependent baby to learn "Cause & Effect"...when I feel pressure, then I release, wet stuff comes out. It informs baby about pee/poo (which has been hidden thus far) and speeds learning. You will also learn his signals and natural timing. WARNING! Please see: Doing Regular Diaper-free Time, Responsibly.

6. **Go for the easy catches first.** At first, rely more on Generic Timing (times when babies commonly have to go). This gets baby and you used to what a "catch" feels like, building confidence. Examples: during diaper change, upon waking, after taking out of carrier, etc.

7. **Mobile babies.** Modify observation time by either doing it over a non-carpet surface, naked-bottomed, and watching closely; or, observe while wearing your baby in a baby carrier.

8. **Wear your baby more often and try co-sleeping.** The closer you are to your baby, the more signals you will catch on to, as well as the natural timing of his pottying needs.

9. **Be sure to write down your baby's Signals and Natural Timing** during your observation periods, no matter how you adapt the observation step. Just don't go overboard! Having a visual record will help you get in tune. Use the Signal and Timing Logs, available in the Readers' Area. Learning natural timing based on feeding and waking is generally easier (which these logs incorporate).

10. **Signals may now equal the "peepee dance."** As baby ages, his signals may equate more and more to your typical childlike "peepee dance," such as fidgeting, jumping around, and getting increasingly hyper and irritable. This is a good thing to learn about your child.

11. **Transport your baby to the potty** if she pees during naked time. Model where the pee and poo go by (gently, calmly) airlifting your little darling to the potty if she should start peeing or pooing during naked observation time. Even if you just catch a drip, that is fine. It will teach her the motion of going to the potty herself. DO IT CALMLY.

12. **Switch from cueing along with baby to prompting** with the words you'd like him to begin using to tell you that he needs to go, such as "I need to pee Mama/Papa" (or use signs).

78

13. **If you choose to use verbal language and sign language** before, during, and after pottying, be consistent & brief.

14. **Experiment** with the Position, Cue, Environment, & even Receptacle. Be open, flexible & creative.

15. **Have an "open door" policy in your family's bathroom.** Let your baby watch you potty and potty with you (I'm on mine, you're on yours). Model where the pee/poo goes, but don't make it a big deal.

16. **Spend time around other children who use the potty**, if possible – whether they have been EC'd or not. It is invaluable for older babies to see other babies (or young children) using the potty instead of a diaper. YouTube is a creative option, too.

17. **Discover what helps your baby relax & focus** on the potty. Sing potty songs, keep a bin of potty-only toys next to her potty, run water in the sink.

18. **Do not hover or hyper-focus** on EC.

19. **Get support.** Visit our private support group. Send our community (and me) your challenges and let the good advice flow.

20. **Be patient** and don't expect immediate results. Don't get frustrated if it takes a while to unlearn going in the diaper…it normally takes several months or more.

21. **Don't compare** yourself with others. Enjoy your baby's personal pace.

22. **Be matter-of-fact about poo and pee.** If you notice yourself showing disgust (or other negative emotions) around poo and bodily fluid messes associated with potty learning (an attitude that is learned through cleaning so many messy diapers), remind yourself that pottying is natural;

everybody poops. Likewise, over-celebrating, ogling over how great he pooped, and even praising can be detrimental to his autonomous desires. Be matter-of-fact, gentle, and avoid being overbearing.

23. **Avoid negative** language, attitude, and stance. Remember, punishment, coercion, anger, and pressure are not part of EC. Reward systems, charts, and M&Ms are also not part of EC (they are forms of coercion, too)…but Communication is. If a wise toddler picks up on any of the more negative or pressuring vibes, it could very well sabotage the whole learning process and delay potty independence. Take a deep breath and seek support if you start losing it (we all do at some point).

24. **Success and order varies.** You may have success with poo first, then pee much later; pee then poo; nighttime then daytime; day then night. Take it as it comes, in whichever order it works.

25. **Delayed signals are normal** for older-starting babies. If he tells you every time after he poos in his pants, don't worry…this is common for late starters. He will eventually start telling you before.

26. **Potty pauses commonly happen** for older starters (although they can happen to any baby). Your child is directly in the middle of so much learning and development, and with illness, teething, travel, and other life changes, potty learning becomes pushed to the end of the list for them. It's also a time for pushing limits, and potty pauses can coincide with toddlerhood. Let him explore and trust him to learn. Model what's expected. Be patient. Read my section on Potty Pauses.

27. **Use "reflective language" & enlist an older baby's help in clean-up.** When your older baby has a miss in the home, state matter-of-factly, "Pee/poo goes in the potty." Then, enlist her help in cleaning it up and taking it to the

bathroom. Be consistent with this. Do not punish; be gentle yet clear in your reflections of what should happen.

28. **Talk about things openly** with your child, when they happen (briefly, yet matter-of-factly: where it goes, how it just went in an undesirable space, where pee/poo belongs, how it feels, his feelings around it, etc.). He can understand more than you think.

29. **Trust your intuition** as it develops. Notice thoughts, images, or sensations that lead you to a hunch that baby needs to go, and act on them.

30. **Trust your baby's growing intuition** as it develops. As she learns about herself, she may want more and more control over the pottying process. Trust her to experiment and learn in her own way. If she insists that she doesn't need to go, or that she can do it herself, listen and give that a chance to be. She will learn from trying to rely on herself.

31. **Read books together** about pottying with your older child.

32. **Get your baby used to sitting on the potty** by sitting him on it while he's still wearing his diaper (if this is a problem for you). As he learns that it's okay and comfortable to sit on the potty, gradually remove the diaper from the equation. Or, if your baby is fine with sitting on the potty but won't go in it just yet, regularly let her spend time sitting on it, getting comfortable with it, without any pressure or agenda.

33. **Enlist the help of family and older children.** Get everyone involved for a very connecting and rewarding family experience. Older children tend to have extra-sensitive intuition around when a baby needs to potty.

POSITIONS GALLERY

THE POSITIONS & OTHER PHOTOS

What's your favorite
EC position?

This section contains a photo series of the main EC positions, a step-by-step photo series for setting up a soaker pad, and additional photos of babies in various positions.

A LITTLE BIT ABOUT EC POSITIONS

There are many ways to position your baby for pottying. Some babies like some positions and resist others. Babies may also change preference from one position to another as time goes on.

Here are some keys for using the positions listed on the following pages.

1. Choose a position that is:
   - comfortable
   - relaxing
   - safe
   - secure
   - supportive (spine, neck, and head)
   - warm (temperature of place, clothing on baby)
   - hygienic.

2. Hold your baby gently with a peaceful, neutral attitude.

3. Be open and experiment until you find a position that meets both of your needs.

4. Use wise, loving, intelligent care while handling your infant.

INDOOR POTTYING POSITIONS

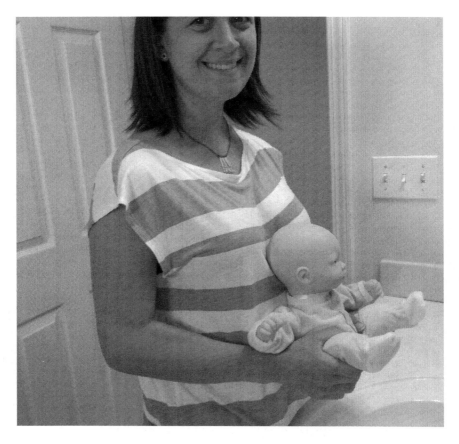

CLASSIC EC POSITION OVER SINK

Hold baby gently under the thighs, resting baby's back, neck, and head on your torso. Also known as a "deep squat" "typical EC hold," and "classic EC hold." This photo shows the position over the sink.

CRADLED CLASSIC EC POSITION OVER SINK

For babies who resist the classic EC position (some don't feel comfortable, safe, or relaxed in it), simply hold the baby by the thighs and rest baby's back, neck, and head in the crook of your bent arm/elbow. Aim the rear end over the sink. This position is great for newborns!

Bottom-back Position Over Sink Part 1

Hold baby under armpits with your hands around ribcage. Place baby's feet on the edge of the sink/counter. If baby is very young, you can scoop your fingers up behind her head to hold it up for her, while still holding her under the armpits with your thumbs. Another nice position for newborns who dislike the classic.

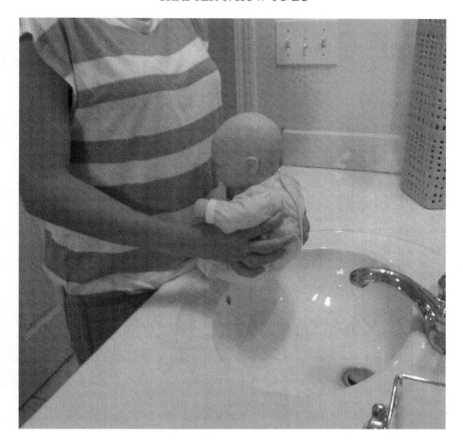

BOTTOM-BACK POSITION OVER SINK PART 2

After positioning baby's feet on the edge of the sink/counter, shift baby's bottom back over the sink to complete the position.

IN-ARMS STANDING POSITION OVER SINK (FOR BOYS)

If your boy dislikes the other holds, the standing, supported hold may be your answer. Hold baby snugly with one hand across his chest/belly and the other hand across his shins (between the knee and feet). Balance his feet on the edge of the sink or counter. His body should be pressed up against your torso. If you need to aim, use the pinky finger of your lower hand to reach up and aim the penis into the sink.

BREASTFEEDING OVER SINK

Especially good for late-night pottying with an infant who has trouble relaxing, but definitely needs to go, the Breastfeeding Over Sink position is kind of an acrobatic act. Basically, you'll do the Cradled Classic EC Position with one additional detail: the baby remains latched to your breast. Don't forget to aim!

91

CLASSIC EC POSITION INTO BATHTUB

This is a good position for a boy or girl who pees straight out - allowing the wall of your bathtub to "catch" the pee! Simply do the Classic EC Position while carefully holding your baby over the bathtub. Be sure baby's neck and head are still supported or baby may not like this position.

BATHTUB TOWEL POSITION

Imagine this photo with a bath towel (not pictured) laid over the edge of the bathtub, underneath the baby. Then, sit the baby on the towel, holding him around the waist, and cue. The pee will spray onto the wall, into the tub, or will soak into the towel, and the towel will keep everyone from slipping around.

Classic EC Position Squatting in Tub

This is the Classic EC Position while standing and squatting inside the tub. For smaller parents and out of some unique necessity (such as a boy who pees straight out), you may try pottying directly in the tub. Be sure baby's head and neck are supported by your torso, and hold underneath the thighs.

CLASSIC EC POSITION SQUATTING IN SHOWER

If you have a stand-up stall shower, this position is great. Some babies like to be close to the ground when they potty. Put the baby into the classic EC position by gently holding the thighs and resting her back, neck, and head against your torso. Squat straight down and use your thighs to "lock in" your baby, which makes her feel secure. This position is commonly used outdoors.

CLASSIC EC POSITION SQUATTING OVER TOILET

Facing the toilet put baby into the classic EC position. Lower into a squat while facing the toilet, tightening your knees and thighs tight around the bowl for stability. Hold your baby over the toilet while resting his body on your chest. Do not hold your baby away from your body in this position. It's not safe and most babies don't like it, as it causes them to feel insecure, as if they are dangling and might fall through the air.

CRADLED CLASSIC EC POSITION SQUATTING OVER TOILET

If your baby resists the classic EC position, try the more relaxed cradled version. Put baby into Cradled Classic position facing the toilet; squat and tighten your knees and thighs around the bowl for stability. Don't hold your baby away from your body. Another good one for the newborns.

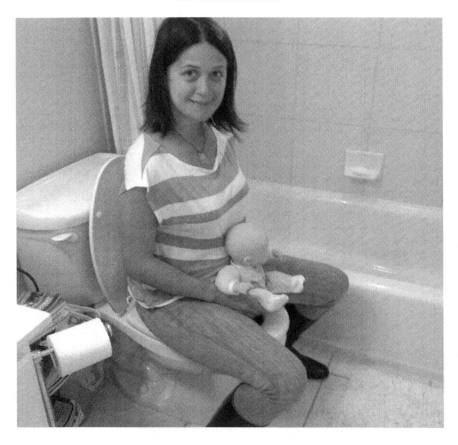

CLASSIC EC POSITION WHILE SITTING BACK ON TOILET

Hold your baby by the thighs with baby's back, neck, and head resting against your body (classic EC position) as you sit far back on the open toilet, leaving a little open space for baby to pee into the toilet.

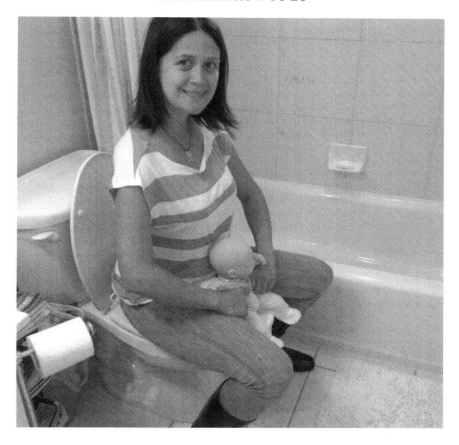

SITTING BACK ON TOILET, HOLDING A SITTING BABY

If your baby can hold her head up pretty well and is close to (or already) sitting, sit far back on the open toilet, leaving a little open space for baby to pee into the toilet. Let your baby sit on the toilet seat and hold her either by the arms or midsection, whichever is most comfortable and secure.

HOLD BABY ON TOILET SEAT FACING YOU

When your baby is able to hold his head up on his own, especially when he's able to sit on his own, this position can be helpful. You can hold your baby around the midsection or by the hands or arms.

HOLD BABY ON TOILET, FACING YOU WITH TOILET SEAT REDUCER

This is the same as above but with the addition of a toilet seat reducer. In general, for girls and boys, toilet seat reducers help a baby feel more comfortable on the big toilet. To contain boy pee, use a toilet seat reducer with a good, tall splashguard, or lean your boy slightly back so his stream has more room.

CLASSIC EC POSITION OVER TOP HAT POTTY

Place the top hat potty in between your legs, squeezing slightly to hold it in place. You can do this while sitting on a chair, in the car, or while sitting on the floor with your legs straight out. Hold your baby by the thighs, resting his back, neck, and head against your chest in classic EC position over the top hat potty.

HOLD BABY ON TOP HAT POTTY, FACING AWAY

This is a great position for use in a parked car, sitting on the floor with your legs straight out, or sitting on a chair. Place the top hat potty in between your legs, squeezing it slightly to hold it in place. Leaning the baby's back, neck, and head against your torso, sit the baby on the top hat potty facing away from you, holding baby around the midsection.

HOLD BABY ON TOP HAT POTTY, FACING TOWARD YOU

This is yet another nice position for use in a parked car, sitting on a chair, or sitting on the floor with your legs straight out. Place the top hat potty in between your legs, squeezing it slightly to hold it in place. Hold the baby around the midsection to help her sit on the top hat potty while facing toward you.

CLASSIC EC POSITION OVER MINI POTTY ON GROUND

Set the mini potty on the floor. Hold baby under thighs and rest his back, neck, and head against your torso (classic EC position). Whether kneeling or sitting, hold baby over the mini potty and aim carefully.

HOLD BABY ON MINI POTTY ON GROUND, FACING AWAY

Sit on the ground with your legs straight out in front of you. Set the mini potty in between your legs, facing away from you. Hold your baby with your hands around her midsection, helping her sit on the potty with your assistance, facing away from you.

HOLD BABY ON MINI POTTY ON GROUND, FACING YOU

Set the mini potty on the ground, facing toward you. Sit down with legs crossed in front of the potty. Hold your baby with your hands around her midsection, helping her sit on the potty with your assistance, facing you.

CLASSIC EC POSITION OVER MINI POTTY ON LAP

Set the mini potty on your lap. Hold baby under thighs and rest his back, neck, and head against your torso (classic EC position). Whether sitting on the ground or on a chair, hold baby over the mini potty and aim carefully.

HOLD BABY ON MINI POTTY ON LAP, FACING AWAY

Sit on the ground with your legs straight out in front of you. Set the mini potty on your lap, facing away from you. Hold your baby with your hands around her midsection, helping her sit on the potty with your assistance, facing away from you.

HOLD BABY ON MINI POTTY ON LAP, FACING YOU

Set the mini potty on your lap, facing toward you. Hold your baby with your hands around her midsection, helping her sit on the potty with your assistance, facing you.

HOLD BABY ON MINI POTTY ON LAP, FACING YOU, FOR AIMING

For a boy who pees straight out, you'll do the same as the last position but sit your boy further back on the potty, which would cause him to slightly lean forward, thus aiming the stream to be better contained by the potty's splashguard up front.

BOTTOM-BACK POSITION OVER PAD, PART 1 OF 2

Lay a waterproof or layered puddle pad on any surface. Hold the baby by the midsection under her armpits (supporting her head with your fingers if needed, while leaving your thumbs under her armpits). Plant her feet on the pad...then...

BOTTOM-BACK POSITION OVER PAD, PART 2 OF 2

...shift the weight of baby's bottom back, away from you, aiming it over the pad. I pottied my first baby in this position for the first 6 weeks (until he had some semblance of neck control and could be sat on his mini potty) because he disliked the classic EC position. I folded over and reused dry areas of the pad for each potty, sometimes catching up to 6 pees on one mat before needing to wash.

OUTDOOR POTTYING POSITIONS

CLASSIC EC POSITION WHILE SQUATTING, IN NATURE

Everyone loves this position! Put your baby into the classic EC position by gently holding his thighs and resting his back, neck, and head against your torso. Squat straight down and use your thighs to "lock in" your baby, which makes him feel secure.

If your more mobile baby tries to crawl or walk off from this exploration-enticing position, try singing a song or saying something to distract him before and during use of this position.

CRADLED CLASSIC EC POSITION, IN NATURE, PART 1 OF 2

This picture shows the shape your supporting arm takes to make the cradled classic EC position work.

CRADLED CLASSIC EC POSITION, IN NATURE, PART 2 OF 2

Hold your baby under the thighs and lay her body onto your arm, allowing her head and neck to be cradled by the crook of your arm/elbow, as shown in Part 1 (above).

BOTTOM-BACK POSITION, IN NATURE/CITY, PART 1 OF 2

Find a curb, stone, or other firm surface to balance your baby's feet on while you pee him. Hold the baby by the midsection under his armpits (supporting his head with your fingers if needed, while leaving your thumbs under his armpits). Balance his feet on the firm surface...then...

BOTTOM-BACK POSITION, IN NATURE/CITY, PART 2 OF 2

...shift the weight of baby's bottom back, away from you, aiming it over the ground or concrete. This is a great position to potty a newborn or smaller baby who dislikes the classic EC position.

THE STRAIGHT LEG POTTY, IN NATURE, PART 1 OF 2

In indigenous tribes, caretakers use this position over the earth to potty younger babies who prefer to potty in this relaxed position. To prepare the "straight leg potty," simply sit down and put your legs straight out with your heels touching each other.

THE STRAIGHT LEG POTTY, IN NATURE, PART 2 OF 2

After you've prepared your straight leg potty, simply lay your baby gently on her back on top of your lower legs, holding her in place with your hands on her upper body, arms, or hands. Your baby should be positioned such that her bottom is over your lower calves/ankles (where a small hole is naturally created when your heels are touching). Her head should be approximately below your knees, her feet at or above your feet.

THE FOOT POTTY, IN NATURE, PART 1 - MAKING THE HOLE

To create a "foot potty," as is done in indigenous tribes around the world, sit with your legs out flat and then slightly bend at the knees, letting your knees fall outward. Put your heels and the balls of your feet together, forming a diamond-shaped hole in the middle. You may need to arch your feet to get a decent-sized hole. Then...

THE FOOT POTTY, IN NATURE, PART 2 - FACING AWAY

...place your baby's bottom directly over the hole you've made, holding her around her midsection, facing away from you. This position is good for a baby with some neck control, but if your baby isn't quite there yet, try facing her toward you, as shown in the next position....

THE FOOT POTTY, IN NATURE, PART 3 - FACING YOU

As mentioned in the last position, if your baby lacks full neck control you can face him toward you, scooping your thumbs under his armpits and using your fingers to balance his head. At any age, set baby on your foot potty with his bottom aimed over the diamond-shaped hole you've made.

Classic EC Position While Squatting, In The City

Put your baby into the classic EC position. Squat straight down and use your thighs to "lock in" your baby, which makes her feel secure. In the cityscape, try to be discreet and only potty your baby where you would potty your dog. Your squat will shield you from most people's views, but when in doubt of offending someone (which does happen!), find a public restroom.

125

CAR POTTYING POSITIONS

CAR POTTYING: CLASSIC EC POSITION OUT THE DOOR

Stop the car in a safe place and get your baby out of his carseat. Still sitting inside the car, carefully hold your baby in the classic EC position, aiming his rear end out the door. Obviously, use caution. This is the way many rural farmers across the world potty their babies, except they do it out of a moving tractor or other vehicle!

CAR POTTYING: CLASSIC EC POSITION SQUATTING BETWEEN CAR DOORS (4-DOOR)

Stop the car in a safe place. For a 4-door car, open both doors on the curb-side of your car. The two doors will shield you from wind and onlookers. Put baby into classic EC position and squat straight down between the doors, "locking" your baby into a secure position between your thighs.

CAR POTTYING: CLASSIC EC POSITION SQUATTING BETWEEN CAR DOORS (2-DOOR)

If you have a 2-door car, open the door on the curb-side of your car. Put baby into classic EC position and squat straight down behind the open door, "locking" her in securely between your thighs.

USING THE TOP HAT POTTY INSIDE PARKED CAR - *SEE THE FOLLOWING*

This is a top hat potty, aka potty bowl, that can be kept in the car at all times or tossed in to your diaper bag for on-the-go pottying. Any time you are somewhere you can sit, this is the best tool for the job (if your baby is small). You hold it in place between your legs. The white thing on top is a potty cozy which keeps the bottom off the cold plastic of the potty. See the Supply List for where to get these unique items.

CLASSIC EC POSITION OVER TOP HAT POTTY, INSIDE CAR

Place the top hat potty in between your legs, squeezing slightly to hold it in place.

Hold your baby by the thighs, resting his back, neck, and head against your chest in classic EC position over the top hat potty.

HOLD BABY ON TOP HAT POTTY, FACING AWAY, INSIDE CAR

This is a great position for use in a parked car. Place the top hat potty in between your legs, squeezing it slightly to hold it in place. Leaning the baby's back, neck, and head against your torso, sit the baby on the top hat potty facing away from you, holding baby around the midsection.

HOLD BABY ON TOP HAT POTTY, FACING TOWARD YOU, INSIDE CAR

This is yet another nice position for use in a parked car. Place the top hat potty in between your legs, squeezing it slightly to hold it in place. Hold the baby around the midsection to help her sit on the top hat potty while facing toward you.

HOLD BABY ON TOP HAT POTTY, TILTED FOR BOY, INSIDE CAR

This is a great position for pottying a boy who pees straight out, in a parked car. Place the top hat potty in between your legs, squeezing it slightly to hold it in place. Leaning the baby's back, neck, and head against your torso, sit the baby on the top hat potty facing away from you, holding baby around the midsection. Tilt the top hat potty toward you as shown in the picture, ensuring your aim is on target!

CRADLED CLASSIC EC POSITION ON TOP HAT POTTY, INSIDE CAR

For babies who resist the classic EC position (some don't feel comfortable, safe, or relaxed in it), simply hold the baby by the thighs and rest baby's back, neck, and head in the crook of your bent arm/elbow. Aim the rear end over the top hat potty, which is held securely between your thighs.

NURSING OVER TOP HAT POTTY INSIDE CAR

Place the top hat potty in between your legs prior to nursing (if you know your baby's Natural Timing is to pee during nursing, or if you know your baby needs to be relaxed into pottying by nursing).

Get your baby into nursing position and rest his or her bottom over the top hat potty opening. If a boy, you may need to tilt the potty a little so the stream goes in. If a girl, try to get her bottom nice and centered.

DUMPING THE TOP HAT POTTY

If your baby just peed in the top hat potty while you're in a parked car, simply pull the lip of the potty cozy down (if you've got one on it) and dump it via the uncovered side, as in the picture. If there's poop in it, save it til you get to a toilet. Or, some people place a medium sized yogurt container inside and pop the lid on the container once it has been filled, dumping it later or throwing the whole thing away right then or later.

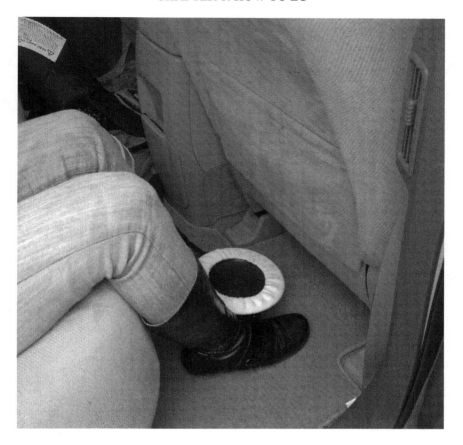

Balancing a Full Top Hat Potty in the Car

I've made the mistake...once...of not securing the used top hat potty on the drive home. If you're not driving, simply hold the top hat in place between your feet as shown in this picture til you get to a place you can dump it. If you are driving, be mindful of putting it somewhere where it won't dump out on the way home.

HOLD BABY ON MINI POTTY ON LAP, FACING YOU, INSIDE CAR

Sit on any open seat in your parked car. Set the mini potty on your thighs, facing toward you. Hold your baby with your hands around his midsection, helping him sit, with your assistance, on the potty. Dump pee outside or save the poop for when you get indoors. Some people place a shallow yogurt container inside and pop the lid on the container once it has been filled.

Classic EC Position Over Mini Potty, Inside Car

Set the mini potty on your lap or in between your thighs. Hold baby under thighs and rest his back, neck, and head against your torso (classic EC position). Hold baby over the mini potty and aim carefully. Or, simply set baby on mini potty facing away from you while sitting in the parked car.

SETTING UP A SOAKER PAD ON ANY SURFACE

PART 1 OF 4

For diaper-free observation time or pottying while breastfeeding, you can set up this easy soaker pad on any surface, including on your body as you lay down with baby laying on you. First, place a waterproof pad (shown), wool puddle pad, piece of 100% wool felt, or towel on the surface you're using.

PART 2 OF 4

Next, place a receiving blanket, cotton blanket, sheet, towel, or other cloth on top of the bottom layer. If you're using a wool puddle pad or felted wool material, liquid will bead up on top of the pad and fall off...so, another layer above this is essential. If you're using a waterproof pad with a top cloth layer, you may choose to skip this step.

PART 3 OF 4

Place a prefold cloth diaper on top of the blanket or cloth.

PART 4 OF 4

For diaper-free observation, lay the baby on top of the prefold cloth diaper with her bottoms off, but dressed warmly otherwise so she is comfortable. Adjust the temperature of the room if necessary.

MODIFICATION FOR OBSERVING BOYS

For a boy who pees upward or straight out, you may want to drape another prefold over his penis. Alternatively, you can place a prefold loosely between his legs and pay attention to when it becomes wet or soiled. However, this may keep you from knowing exactly when he pees or poos, and may prevent you from easily spotting his pre-potty signals.

BREASTFEEDING POTTYING POSITIONS

NURSING POSITION OVER SOAKER PAD OR TOP HAT POTTY

Assume the feeding position, leaving your baby's bottom uncovered but keeping her warm with long socks or leg-warmers. You will keep her over the pad or aimed over the top hat potty while feeding. With a boy, you can drape a prefold over his penis to keep dry.

CRADLED CLASSIC EC POSITION OVER SOAKER PAD

When baby pops off your breast or becomes still (whatever her signal is), you can either leave her in feeding position & cue (last photo) or use this one. Simply keep the arm that baby is resting on to breastfeed where it is & slide that hand under her outer thigh, moving your other hand to support her inner thigh. You'll shift to gently holding both thighs and keep the baby cradled by your breast as you cue.

CLASSIC EC POSITION OVER SOAKER PAD

Alternatively you can transfer baby from feeding position to the classic EC position once he signals you during feeding (by popping off or stopping). Hold baby by the thighs, with his body resting on yours, over the pad. Switch out the pad, top layer, or wet or soiled prefold cloth diaper once he's finished. Learn more about how to potty while breastfeeding in the Unique Situations section of this book.

AIMING THE BOY POTTYING POSITIONS

I've shifted my index finger toward his penis and will use this finger to aim the stream into the sink.

AIMING THE BOY: CLASSIC EC POSITION

Put your baby into classic EC position by holding him under his thighs and resting his back, neck, and head on your torso. Slide one of your hands toward his penis and use your index finger to gently aim his penis toward its destination. Avoid touching his penis after he's already begun peeing, as this can cause him to stop peeing.

AIMING THE BOY: LETTING HIM PRACTICE HIS AIM

Baby boys naturally handle their own penises...regularly. Part of this is instinctually related to stretching the foreskin (whether intact or not); part of this is learning how to aim his pee stream. Allow this so he may learn how to aim it. If pee is going everywhere, do this over the bathtub, outside, or place a mat underneath.

AIMING THE BOY: ON THE MINI POTTY OR TOILET SEAT REDUCER

If the splash guard on your mini potty or toilet seat reducer just isn't tall enough to do its job, here's the fix. Scoot your boy a little further back on the seat. Lean his body gently toward you (toward the front of the seat). This should provide enough angle to get the pee inside.

AIMING THE BOY: ON THE TOP HAT POTTY

Place the top hat potty between your legs. While holding your baby in a seated position, facing away from you, directly on the top hat potty, let go of his thighs and hold the rim of the potty directly. Then, tilt the potty so the opening comes toward you, providing an angle that will help get the pee into the potty. The potty will no longer be held between your legs but instead will come off them just a bit.

AIMING THE BOY: IN THE SHOWER

As mentioned earlier in this photo collection, you can potty your baby in the shower in classic EC position. With a boy, I would just turn around and face the wall so the pee stream would be contained!

AIMING THE BOY: OUTSIDE

As mentioned earlier in this photo series, you can potty your baby outside in classic EC position while squatting. Simply aim your boy in the direction you'd like him to pee!

AIMING THE BOY: AT THE BATHTUB

Place a towel on the edge of the bathtub - this will absorb some of the pee if it trickles down and also serves to create a non-slip surface. Set the baby in a seated position on the towel, facing the tub, with his body supported by your hands and/or body. Cue him. Some of the stream may soak the towel while some may go into the tub or onto the wall.

AIMING THE BOY: INTO A MASON JAR

Holding your baby on your lap, cradled in your arms, or in any comfortable position, hold a small Mason jar, plastic water bottle, or any appropriately-sized vessel near his penis and cue. Do this with a prefold or towel in your lap in case the spray doesn't make it into its destination.

OTHER POSITION PHOTOS

Newborn in Classic EC Position over mini potty.

This baby is not happy because her Papa is holding her in a way that makes her feel insecure. She is not aligned with or supported by the center of his body. He should support her with his body and hold her close to his chest, not out over the potty.

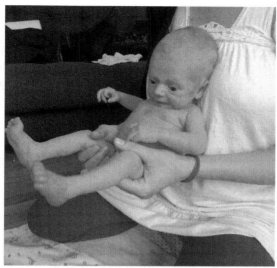

This is a teeny-tiny newborn baby in Classic EC Position over a waterproof mat.

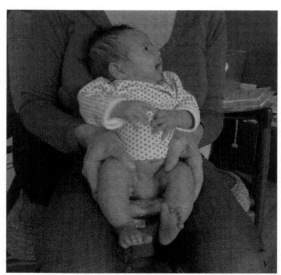

This newborn is being held in Classic EC Position over a top hat potty held between her mother's legs.

157

My first being held in Classic EC Position over a public sink.

My boy being held in Classic EC Position while I squat at the big toilet.

My boy being held in Classic EC Position while I squat at the big toilet.

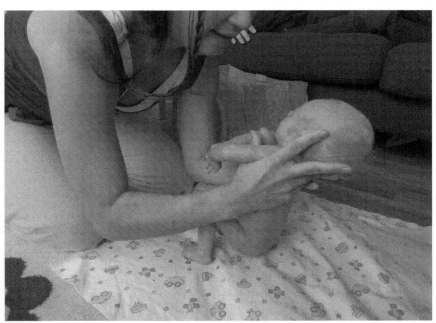

This is a very tiny newborn being held in Bottom-back Position over a waterproof pad, shifting baby's body away so he doesn't pee on his feet, cradling his tiny head with my fingers.

159

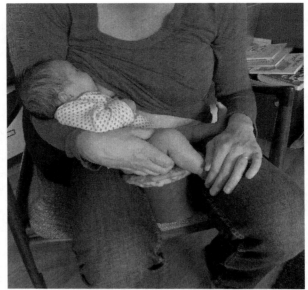

Nursing a newborn with the top hat potty held between Mama's legs, ready for the expected pee/poo, with a warm cozy on the potty.

Pottying my boy in the car on a cold day, I'm holding him in a sitting position, facing away from me, over the portable top hat potty.

My boy at around 6 weeks old, when he had a little neck control but couldn't sit unassisted. A blanket covers his lap early in the cold morning as he goes in the mini potty, which is sitting between my legs on the bed.

This was my boy's first try at the mini potty at 6 weeks old. I got a potty cozy soon after, as he hated the cold plastic.

My boy sitting on his mini potty at 9 months old, with Mama sitting on the big toilet to demonstrate. I'm signing "potty" to him while saying "Peepee" as the Cue to release. His basket of toys are nearby in case we need them.

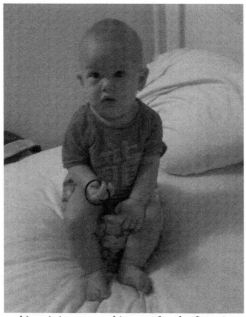

My boy sitting on his mini potty on his own for the first time, on the bed. The flowery thing is his warm potty cozy.

162

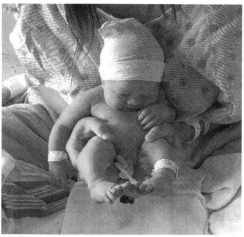

Catching my girl's first meconium poo, on a pad, on the day of her birth.

Pottying my girl at 3 days old in Classic EC Position over the top hat potty while sitting.

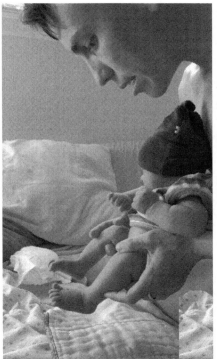

Daddy's first potty with our baby girl at two days old. She began to fuss and he put her in Classic EC Position over a cloth prefold.

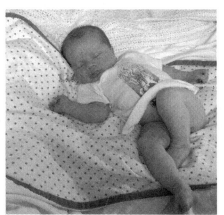

Naked observation time with our newborn girl, over a Kushies waterproof pad (see Supply List for source).

Grandma learning how to EC my daughter, Isadora.

CHAPTER 2:
UNIQUE SITUATIONS + HOW-TO'S

7 UNIQUE SITUATIONS

You will often find yourself in a situation that requires a unique and creative pottying solution.

This page will teach you Unique Situations you may need to know to potty your baby or young toddler, in various situations and times, including:

1. Pottying While Breastfeeding
2. Pottying In Nature
3. City Pottying
4. Car Pottying (Next to Parked Car)
5. Car Pottying (Inside Parked Car)
6. Cold Weather ECing
7. Travel and EC

Keep reading for tips on all of these topics....

POTTYING WHILE BREASTFEEDING

Some babies potty (pee, poo, or both) during breastfeeding, some right after. If this happens to be part of your baby's natural timing, here's what to do:

1. Hold a bowl between your legs during breastfeeding. It can be anything ranging from a mixing bowl to a Tupperware container to a top hat potty that was designed to be held nicely between the legs while sitting (see Supply List). or... Spread a "soaker pad" over your lap while nursing.

For a step-by-step photo demonstration of how to set up a soaker pad on your lap, see the Positions Gallery.

2. Nurse your baby diaper-free or at least dressed in easy-off bottoms, being sure to warm up the room and/or dress the baby in EC-friendly clothing on the legs and upper body.

3. When you notice that your baby "pops off the breast" (she just can't keep her latch), becomes still, or some other signal happens, offer a pottytunity either in the container or over the pad.

4. Position your baby and cue. Many mothers cue their babies while still in breastfeeding position, ensuring the bowl or pad is under the baby's bum.

Others switch to the classic EC position and make the cue, returning the baby to feeding once complete.

Still others choose to modify the classic EC position into the cradled version by keeping baby's little head in the crook of their elbow and moving the hands to hold baby's thighs over the bowl or pad.

In any position, baby will get used to this as an okay place/way to eliminate.

For photos of positions you can use while breastfeeding, see the Positions Gallery.

Don't do anything super-disturbing during breastfeeding. This should be a time of peace and quiet for both of you, with little distraction.

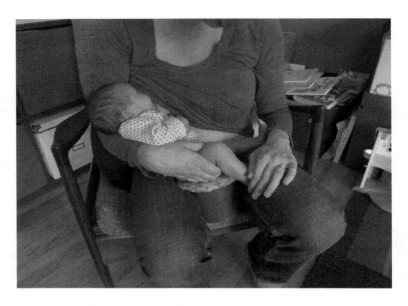

If pottying during breastfeeding is a challenge, nurse your baby diaper-free over a pad or in a loosely fitted diaper and simply <u>cue along with her</u>. This will at least strengthen the sound association and overall communication between you. Constant peeing & pooing during breastfeeding may end (or lessen in frequency) in a few months as your baby matures, so do not fret. This too shall pass....

NOTE: I use the term " breastfeeding" throughout this book, but I mean to lump bottle-feeding into this term, too (my apologies to anyone whom this offends). I know plenty of mothers who either choose not to or are unable to breastfeed, and they are some of the most incredible mothers I know.

If you notice that your baby signals to potty during bottle-feeding, please follow the instructions in this section as well. Popping off the bottle occurs, after all, for the same reasons as popping off the breast. When we give our baby girl pumped breastmilk in a bottle this definitely happens.

POTTYING IN NATURE

People sometimes think ECing in public outdoor places is not sanitary, so you can drum up some nasty looks (or curious ones that lead to great conversations).

Use your highest wisdom and never potty your baby where you wouldn't let your beloved canine urinate or poo. Generally, if there is a public restroom nearby, use it (classic EC position over sink or toilet, cleaning as necessary).

If there is no restroom in sight and you don't have a portable potty with you, but there is a good spot to potty in nature, go for it! But be sure to **be discreet** and **clean up after yourself**.

Follow the normal pottying steps I've already outlined. The only modification is that you are going to hold baby over grass, dirt, or some other natural surface. When baby is held in position and cued, he will generally go in any environment (so long as he needs to go).

A big variable here is the weather…if it's too cold, baby may protest and you'll either have to shield him from the breeze or remember to dress him in long socks underneath those pants next time (see our Supply List).

Another variable is distractability. If you have a mobile baby who wants to crawl off when held over the ground, say or sing something to distract him as you matter-of-factly (but gently) position him & squat.

The best position to use in nature is the classic EC position while you are squatting yourself (below). Your legs shield him from wind and others' sight, and he feels safe against your chest with your body surrounding him.

171

However, for a very young baby you can alternatively face him to you, "stand" him on a stone or surface, lean his rear back (help him sit into the position), and then cue him. I call this the bottom-back position (below).

For more photos of positions you can use in nature, see the Positions Gallery.

With pee there's no need to clean up. It will evaporate and it's even a little cleaner than dog pee (which is constantly deposited in nature).

With poop, however, you will need to clean up. If baby is still breastfeeding and thus poo is runny, simply cover it with other natural material (like soil, leaves, or grass). If baby's poo is more solid, you may want to carry bags with you (Biobags are biodegradable & available in pet supply stores) and throw it away properly (as you would with a dog).

Not that I'm comparing your baby with a dog!

City Pottying

EC in the city is very similar to EC in nature. The main differences are that there are more people around, cars and buses scooting by, and delightful concrete instead of grass. Be discreet and be sure to clean up after yourself!

Again, if you can find a public restroom, potty your baby over the sink or toilet (hold over receptacle in the classic EC position) and clean as necessary. If not, time to get creative....

I've pottied my son on a discreet part of the sidewalk/alley before when none of the nearby shops had a public bathroom.

If there's grass nearby and not a huge crowd of people, we go there. But sometimes in San Francisco there is no grass and we have to potty city-style.

CAR POTTYING (NEXT TO PARKED CAR)

I've sometimes pottied my son on the side of the road or in a parking lot if I've forgotten the portable top hat potty…so I choose to go next to the car.

All you have to do, with a 4-door vehicle, is open both doors on the curb-side of the car so you are somewhat shielded from sight (with a 2-door just open the one door). You can sit on the seat inside the car and hold baby over the concrete in the classic EC position and cue. Or, better yet, you can get out of the car too and squat with baby (in between the two open doors, or behind the one open door) while putting her into position and cueing.

If the outdoor cityscape is not amenable to pottying, try inside the car….

CAR POTTYING (INSIDE PARKED CAR)

Sometimes we pull over to potty our son and it's really cold outside. What could have been a nature or city pee becomes an inside-the-car pee.

We travel with a portable top hat potty (see our Supply List) that fits in between our legs. I highly recommend this. If not, have a mini potty, bowl, tupperware, or other container in the car handy (even a frisbee works...yes, we've tried it!).

To potty in the car, simply pull over, put the potty between your legs, at the ready, and get the baby out of the carseat. Remove her pants and diaper/undies (if any) while telling her that you are going to go pee-pee, so she knows what to expect.

For more photos of positions you can use in the city and in and around the car, see the Positions Gallery.

Hold your baby over the potty either facing you or facing away and cue. If baby is a little older and very distractable, simply hold her in the classic EC hold over the potty so her weight is in your hands. Be sure to aim well...especially with boys! (Some people have a water bottle or jar handy in the car just for this boy-friendly occasion.)

After pottying, set the potty on the floor of the car temporarily, being careful not to spill it. Lay baby sideways on your lap and put on the diaper (if any) and pants.

Put baby back in car seat and then (if you have a warming potty cozy on it) pull down the lip of the cozy and dump the pee out the door. If it's poo too, dispose of it more sanitarily (ie: keep a plastic bag in the car, or even place a to-go container in the potty and box up the treasure for later disposal). If you can't dispose of either, place a cloth in there to soak it up. Or...

Sometimes I hold the potty between my feet on the floorboard to ensure it doesn't spill on the way home & I empty it there.

COLD WEATHER ECING

If you live in a colder climate or your baby is tiny during a colder season, you can still practice EC successfully. Don't put it off til it's warm…you may miss a vital window of opportunity!

First, try to keep the climate within your home comfortable for everyone, as babies generally need to be warmer than we do. If there's a way to provide diaper-free time inside by occasionally warming the thermostat, do it…it's worth the learning experience for both of you. But remember…do naked time responsibly!

Next, dress the baby in EC-friendly layers. If you must bundle up indoors, layer long socks with leg-warmers, then cover those all with wool socks and pants. Invest in wool…it enables you to use less layers. Use longer t-shirts and jackets/hoodies. Avoid the huge snowman onesie unless you need to go outside in the snow or freezing weather. Use an easy-on, easy-off diapering system if you choose to use a diaper back-up.

When our family was camping in the Northwest US, I discovered that using split-crotch pants or chaps covered in a cloth diaper & diaper cover made for a seamless, warm, gentle middle-of-the-night potty. Under the pants I used Rock-a-Thigh Baby socks and my babe was super-cozy for the midnight pee.

See my Supply List for places I've found that carry the best of these items.

Lastly, when out and about, bring a top hat or mini potty with you so you can potty within the warmth of you car and avoid pottying outdoors. Or find a public bathroom and utilize it. If your baby is in warm yet EC-friendly layers, he won't mind having them removed for a quick pee. But if it's really cold, always have a warm place in mind just in case (like your car).

The Eskimos reportedly would have their babies pee or poo into a container and then toss the refuse outdoors into the wild. If you live in a situation like that (or perhaps are camping), might as well try it!

178

TRAVEL AND EC

15 TIPS FOR PRACTICING EC DURING TRAVEL

1. **Always locate the potty first.** When entering the airport, a restaurant, or a shop, find the potty and offer a pottytunity first (if appropriate), then enjoy what you're there to do.

2. **Use a back-up when you anticipate stress (or lack of potties).** This can even be a disposable diaper...it won't ruin your progress with EC if you normally use cloth or underwear. Everyone will be happier if you use something at a time when you're likely to need it.

3. **Wear your baby.** You will be more in-touch with his signals and he will be more likely to hold it while you find the proper receptacle/potty place.

4. **Bring a small mini potty with you.** Instead of filling your carry-ons with diapers, you can fit a small mini potty into the bag. Most airlines allow for a diaper bag as a bonus carry-on.

179

Use it at your seat when that seatbelt sign prevents you from using the lavatory on the plane. Otherwise, hold your baby in-arms over the lavatory toilet or sink when it's time to go.

5. **Be discreet and clean up after yourselves.** Don't just pee your baby anywhere because you're in a 3rd world country (and especially not if you're in a Westernized one). Most people prefer that you use the proper facilities. If you have to potty in nature, be sure to clean up so the remains don't attract wild animals.

6. **Pack only what you need.** You'd be surprised…EC on the road can sometimes be a lot more efficient than it is at home. No one is bored, everyone is in the present moment and connected to immediate needs, things move more smoothly. Bring the minimum of things and know that you can grab extra gear in most places along the way. Just remember that you'll probably be more attuned to your baby while traveling, and that misses are normally going to be only pees if you're paying attention and baby is simply adjusting. Most babies don't like to soil pants in places where they aren't familiar with people or things.

7. **At every new place of lodging, set up that potty station FIRST.** Show your baby to it, offer the potty, and generally get settled in. Whether at a hotel or in a tiny bungalow, having a little potty station is quite key.

8. **On airplanes, request the bulkhead/bassinet seats when available.** Especially on a long international flight, you'll appreciate both the bassinet and the legroom! It's priceless to have the room to set your potty on the carpet and potty your kiddo there while the (sometimes eternally-on) stay in your seat light is bright. You can usually request these seats when you book your flights. Even airlines that no longer assign seats ahead of time will make an exception for those with lap babies.

9. **For those who practice nighttime EC, set up your array of tools in your sleep space like you would at home.** Try to emulate the home night pottying environment as much as possible. Again, pack light, but also try to make things easy and familiar during those wee hours of potty time.

10. **Always potty your baby when YOU need to go to the bathroom.** Whether you're at the in-laws or in a restaurant, it's good practice to always bring baby with you and offer (if you can hold her and do your business at the same time, then switch!). It will help you remember to stay attuned to her needs, and often we need to go at the same time.

11. **For the baby-pass-around at family or friends' homes, use a back-up on your baby** OR pay attention to how much time has passed and take your baby to pee at the usual intervals (based on your baby's natural, usual potty rhythms, if you know them by now). If it's too much to socialize and pay attention, or you don't want to draw "odd" attention to yourself, simply use a back-up. It won't ruin your practice to occasionally do this.

12. **Stay consistent, catch the easy ones, and stay in tune with your own intuition.** Don't just drop EC because you're on vacay. That is what screws things up when traveling, not the traveling itself! Keep doing your wake up and pees, your diaper change pottytunities, and your potty-upon-arrival "easy catches." Pay attention to when that little voice in your head says "it's time." And also pay attention to when potty paranoia is mistaken for potty intuition...if you're nervous about having a miss in public, use a back-up diaper or underwear. Plain and simple.

13. **If you have a bunch of wet ones in a row...remember that you're traveling!** Baby is adjusting to new environments on a more acute level than you are. Don't get frustrated and don't give up. Gather new information from any possible spree of misses and adjust your game. Your EC practice will definitely get back on track when you return home, given you stay consistent and seek support if/when necessary (like in our Private Support Group). Usually misses while traveling indicate that baby is adjusting to the new environment...no need to freak out about it. Just find ways to make it "home" and press on.

14. **While driving or doing an extended road trip, always potty before getting in the car and at every stop, if appropriate.** If you simply can not stop to potty your baby (and you expect this ahead of time), just say "go ahead and go in your diaper and I'll change you at the next stop." Some babies won't have it and will make you pull over. Have a potty ready in the car. Other babies will understand and oblige. It just depends on temperament.

15. **If you pack a cloth back-up, you can easily hand-wash pee diapers in the sink and hang to dry, without soap** (unless super-ammonia-y). Pack about 20 cloth prefolds (newborn size) and 2 covers and use my Quick EC Diapering Method for an easy way to use a back-up while on the go with a baby less than 9-14 months (ie: still using diapers as a back-up) if you want to avoid using disposables on your trip. But, again, if you do choose disposables, don't sweat it. Get back to cloth when you return (if you do cloth). No worries. Nothing will "un-teach" what they've already learned.

NIGHTTIME EC

INTRODUCTION

You may choose to do EC at night or you could skip it altogether. If you want to go for it, this special section will help.

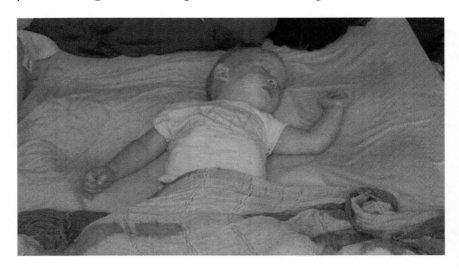

I personally believe that nighttime EC is important...**but only if it provides *everyone* in the family with more restful sleep.** Some babies will become dry at night naturally after achieving daytime dryness through successful daytime EC...with no nighttime EC practice at all! Some will wet that back-up every night til 36 months comes along.

It really depends.

My suggestion for you: give nighttime EC a good, solid try...and ONLY keep doing it if it provides you all with better sleep.

KEY POINTS + HOW-TO'S

NIGHT-WAKING IS SOMETIMES ABOUT NEEDING TO PEE/BE CHANGED

Some parents complain, "I can't get him to sleep through the night!" through red, bagged eyes. Well, newborn babies do not sleep through the night (many report that by 12 weeks they are capable, if you take certain steps in sleep teaching...I'm not talking Cry-It-Out, but there are ways I've heard of that do work...by then. But not at newborn age.). Newborns wake every few hours because they're hungry and...you guessed it...they need to relieve themselves. (This can range from a stretch of up to 2-6 hours of dry sleep, from newborn up to age 12 weeks.)

Generally, babies do not poo at night (early in the morning is common, though). But peeing (especially if you are night-nursing) happens every so often. At first, it will be impossible to catch them all. As baby begins consolidating his pees, it becomes more and more a possibility...ultimately ending in a child who does sleep through the night, dry.

EATING & SLEEPING BOTH TRUMP NIGHT POTTYING

When in doubt, always offer feeding prior to pottying. In the middle of the night, babies voice their upset very clearly if you try to potty them when they're hungry. Eating trumps pottying.

The order in which things happen at night can make starting nighttime EC a tricky task (do I feed first, then potty, then feed more?). We have found that our son really enjoys his sleep (as do we!), so I offer him breastmilk first when he gets squirmy, sometimes switching breasts to give him a fresh one, and if he settles back to sleep, I let him be.

If he continues to squirm (or even yell out, cry, or crawl up to the headboard now that he's older), I offer him the potty.

187

Nap with Your Baby During the Day to Feel More Rested, Overall

This sub-section is mostly for parents with newborns (and for exhausted parents of older infants).

To make waking a few times a night to EC (or just do nighttime parenting) a realistic endeavor, it's vital that you nap with your newborn baby (at the same time, or better yet, in the same bed) every time you can.

During her nap, it's not time to catch up on housekeeping or those nagging unopened emails…it's time for you, the parents, to rest, too!

Trust me, if you nap when she naps, especially in the first 6 months, you will be a happier parent and your baby will get a higher level of presence from you, which we know she deserves. Everything will be less frustrating (especially EC!).

Go to Sleep at the Same Time as Your Baby

When you both go to sleep at the same time, you will be on the same rhythm. Tune yourself into your baby at night by falling asleep with him.

When he shifts to nurse, you will shift right there with him. If he continues to wriggle to ask to pee, you will not be overtired from having had less sleep than him...you'll be in sync and nighttime EC will be much easier.

And, in the daytime, you will feel more rested having had the longer, overall sleeping range with a few wake-ups sprinkled in (as opposed to your pre-baby normal amount of sleep with the wake ups). (And you can always get up early.)

Example: You both go to bed at 8pm, waking in the morning at 7am. That's 11 total hours. You got up 3 times to nurse and pee, equalling 30 minutes of disrupted sleep each time. 11 hours minus 1.5 hours = **9.5 hours** = a great night's sleep for a new parent!!

Alternatively: Baby goes to bed at 8pm; you go to bed at 12 midnight; you both wake at 7am. You get 7 total hours of sleep, but you also got up 3 times to nurse and pee, equalling 30 minutes of disrupted sleep each time. Not to mention, you missed every pee! That's 7 hours minus 1.5 hours = **5.5 hours** = a horrible night's sleep for a new parent!

We always have more misses when my baby and I do not go to sleep at the same time. I either don't hear/feel his signals as well or I am just plain too tired to wake to potty him. I get lazy. And I'm way grouchier the next day.

TIP: If you do want some "alone" time after baby drifts off, I recommend that you stay up no later than a 1/2 hour beyond the time your baby goes down. Wind yourself down by doing some peaceful meditation or reading and then nourish your body with good, long sleep, in sync with your baby's nighttime rhythms. Have your partner pitch in to help the older ones off to sleep...if their bedtime is later.

189

To Co-sleep or Not?

With a newborn, and an infant of any age, the goal is for everyone in the family to maximize the amount and quality of sleep they get.

You may get this with baby sleeping in the other room, in your room, or snuggled right up against mom. Sharing sleep is uber-controversial in modern day society, but parents the world over do it safely, and parents in the Western world are returning to the natural wisdom of co-sleeping in greater numbers every day.

Point is: if your baby (and everyone else) sleeps best in your bed, by all means, do it. Research it, make it safe, and do it if it feels right for your family.

Regarding your EC practice, co-sleeping absolutely helps you do nighttime EC. Your baby is designed to wriggle and complain when she needs nighttime help, and you are **designed** to wake easily to these signals and come to her aid.

For the research, see Dr. Sears' Attachment Parenting book.

Advice for Non-Co-sleepers

If she's in the other room, or even separated from you in your room, it's going to be a bit more challenging to discern her needs, and with EC, you may have a miss if she's waking to potty. Some parents put the crib or bassinet in the room with them so they can hear the baby and attend to her needs more quickly, and with less disruption of sleep…but again the response time is somewhat compromised compared to sharing the bed.

The solution for ECing when your baby sleeps in a separate space? Two options may work for you:

1. Offer pottytunities <u>during nighttime diaper changes</u>. When your baby wakes you in the night, go to her quickly. Offer her a pottytunity whether her diaper is wet or not. A wet-diapered-baby may be holding the next pee for a chance to potty elsewhere…or if she's dry, she may have been waiting for you. Keep a potty handy next to the changing table.

2. Offer pottytunities based on <u>Timing</u>. Some suggested nighttime pottytunities include:
   - pottying last thing before bedtime,
   - setting an alarm to wake baby a few hours later,
   - another alarm a few hours after that, followed by
   - a morning pee right after waking.

How to know what time to set the alarms? Well, you might just have to sleep with your baby a night or two to find out (or sleep in her room if it's separate from you and you don't feel comfy with her in your bed).

Or, you could write down when she wakes you to change a wet diaper, noticing a pattern over the course of a few days, and then set your alarm to wake up *right before* that usual time.

IF YOU <u>DO</u> CO-SLEEP

If you do co-sleep, you may find it easier to potty at night.

How to potty at night if co-sleeping? Generally, if you are sleeping curled up with your baby, he will wriggle around and maybe whimper or cry when he needs to go (or even yell out, cry, or crawl up to the headboard when older), or perhaps some nights he signals when he goes because he's just plain tired. Some nights he may want to sleep and not potty; some he may want a dry diaper all night.

Remember to offer food first, then see if he settles, and if not, offer the potty.

NIGHT-NURSING AND NIGHTTIME EC

Night-nursing certainly helps baby relax to potty and then go back to sleep with ease, but it is not necessary. Some women are physically unable to nurse, and some choose to not nurse during the night and/or to ween early.

If are you are able and/or willing to night-nurse, I encourage you to do it. Not only does it help baby sleep, but it's very handy for when baby won't potty unless you're simultaneously nursing.

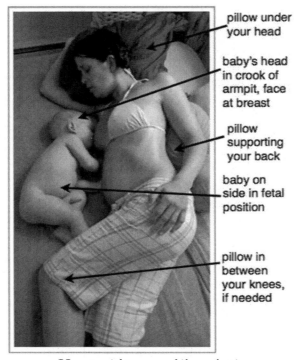

pillow under your head

baby's head in crook of armpit, face at breast

pillow supporting your back

baby on side in fetal position

pillow in between your knees, if needed

How to night-nurse while co-sleeping

According to Dr. Sears, babies will leave the family bed, and wean from night-nursing, eventually on their own...and they state that contrary to popular belief, these practices do not make a dependent, needy baby. See his book for more information.

HOW TO PROTECT YOUR BED

Layer a cloth mattress pad (not rubber or plastic which make baby sweat profusely) over the mattress, topped by a wool puddle pad, topped by a fitted cotton sheet, topped by you and your baby, topped by your blankets.

When you have a miss, simply put a cloth diaper directly on the pee puddle on the sheet and the diaper will soak the pee into itself without leaving a trace on the sheet or the bed below.

Here is a photo-by-photo demonstration of how to set up your bed protection:

Start with a bare mattress...then add...

a cloth mattress pad (not rubber or plastic),

a wool puddle pad or piece of 100% wool felt,

a fitted sheet, and lastly…

a cotton prefold diaper placed over a miss to absorb the pee out of the sheet and wool…after a few hours, the sheet & wool will be dry and you will only have to wash the diaper.

NIGHT POTTYING TROUBLESHOOTING

Your baby may be content with pottying at night in earlier months...and then it may change. A royal struggle breaks out every time he signals but resists the act of pottying. He'd rather be asleep, but he's not able to rest because he needs to pee.

What to do when night pottying becomes a challenge?

1. Be sure the lighting where you potty your baby is dimmed.
2. Be sure the temperature in the room is comfortable. Put a warm potty cozy on your potty if you use one.
3. Minimize the amount of clothing you'll need to remove, but make sure baby is still cozy in what's left.
4. Experiment with letting your baby sleep diaper-free (over a soaker pad), in undies, in training pants, or in diapers (cloth or disposable) to see what most invokes your baby's instincts to signal and pee. Every baby differs.
5. Try nursing first, before pottying.
6. Try nursing while pottying baby, whether he is over the sink, on the top hat potty or mini potty, or naked over a pad. It may take some balancing to nurse and potty at the same time...but some babies can only relax enough in this way. Cue while you nurse to encourage him to release.
7. Go to sleep at the same time your baby does, no more than a 1/2 hour later. Trust me, you will be 100% more in-tune with and able to respond to nighttime pottying signals if you do this, feeling more rested and patient, too.
8. Nap with your younger baby when she naps during the day. Resist "getting things done" and rest up yourself! This makes nighttime parenting easier.
9. If you find that you're missing a lot at night, it could mean that you're doing too much during the day. If you can, cut back on stress-creators like extra work, chores, and errands. Ask others to help you out during the day so that you don't spend all your sleeping hours recovering (and not in-tune with baby).
10. Try giving baby a bath before going to sleep at night. This will help her more easily float into deep sleep and feel more rested when she wakes to nurse/pee.

11. Try a new position, receptacle, and/or environment. Try going from a normal sitting on the mini-potty position to turning the potty around and holding baby in the classic EC position, leaning baby's body up against your chest for nighttime support. Try pottying baby in the bathroom over the sink in cradled classic EC position, or close to the ground next to your bed over a wide, shallow tray or bin.

12. If you think baby is signaling, yet he's resisted night pottying in the near past, simply feed him and see if he goes back to sleep. He may wait until the next time when he is really ready to wake up and potty. He may have learned that he can now hold it longer. He may be teething, sick, or going through a growth spurt and too tired to budge. If he goes back to sleep, let him be til he really asks for it.

13. Talk to the baby who is giving obvious potty signals to wake him up a bit before offering the potty. Say something gently, softly, such as, "Do you need to go peepee?" or "I'm going to take you to the bathroom" while touching him lightly. Don't worry, your stimulation won't ruin rest time. After relieving himself and getting a clean diaper, he will likely fall right back to sleep...easily.

14. Sing quietly to the baby who fusses when night pottied. Oftentimes this will relax him and even if he continues to fuss he will probably pee with the song. (We like "Twinkle, Twinkle.")

15. If you've been pottying on the bed (in potty or on pad) and it no longer works, bring baby to the bathroom and offer her the sink or toilet under dimmed lighting. Some babies will begin to prefer to eliminate where the grown-ups go...in the bathroom...even during the night! Peeing on the bed (even though it's in a potty or on a mat) may begin to feel counter-instinctual (remember, they don't want to soil their bed).

16. If your baby sleeps naked or in undies and regularly pees on the bed, and it's happening too often for your nerves or intuitive sense to handle...put that baby in a cloth diaper back-up! **You are teaching him to wet the bed.** Don't let pride of having a "diaper-free baby" get in the way of your sanity...and sense. "Diaper-free" means free from dependence upon diapers, not naked-peeing-everywhere-even-at-night.

17. If all else fails, temporarily pause nighttime pottying. If baby begins to ask for it again, follow his lead and offer it. If baby would rather sleep, it is probably better for everyone's sleep to just let him be. If you choose to stop night pottying altogether, see the following sub-section, below, for tips on doing so.

18. If you stop or pause nighttime EC, focus on your daytime EC and trust that your baby will eventually integrate this learning into her nighttime routine.

IF YOU CHOOSE NOT TO NIGHT POTTY

If offering the potty at night disturbs either of your sleep to unlivable, stressful proportions, I say don't do it. Often night dryness follows day dryness much later.

For now, either switch to cloth diapers at night OR use a modified disposable diaper (with a piece of cut-up washcloth in it, see below). Change your baby if/when she wakes you, and get on with your sleep.

After looking at statistics in America that showed cloth-diapered babies of the 1940's were potty independent by 12-18 months, and after speaking to a native Mexican mother who told me her kids were dry at night by 12 months because they used cloth at night…I do suggest cloth.

"But, Andrea, cloth diapering is foreign, expensive, scary, and a lot of work!!"

I know, it seemed that way to me at first, too! See my advice on super-easy-to-use, inexpensive cloth diapering here: How to Diaper with EC.

"But I really want to continue using disposable diapers, Andrea!"

No problem. If you want to continue using disposables, add the washcloth insert and/or change your baby's diaper frequently throughout the night (again, see: How to Diaper with EC).

Finally, if none of this works for you, you can (of course!) just deal with nighttime potty training later. I want you to be a happy, rested parent!

HOW I'VE DONE OUR NIGHTTIME ROUTINES, STAGE BY STAGE

I hope that sharing my nighttime EC journey with you will help you in some way. I've certainly tried most everything.

Our Newborn Night Pottying Routine (0-4 months)
When my first baby was little bitty, he hated the classic EC position so I created what I call Bottom-back Position (see the Positions Gallery) and peed him at night on the leftover disposable pads from my homebirth.

He'd pee on the pad, I'd fold it over, and re-use the dry area for the next one. He peed so much at this age that <u>I relied heavily on offering pottytunities at all nighttime</u> **diaper changes**...I'd wake up when he was fussing about being wet and offer him a pottytunity before putting on a fresh diaper. He peed every time.

When I ran out of left over disposable pads to pee him on, I invested in some cloth/plastic ones (see our Supply List) and did the same position until he was 6 weeks old and could sit on the Baby Bjorn Smart Potty (BBSP) with my help. I immediately got a potty cozy to wrap it in warmth, as our baby hated a cold seat.

Admittedly, I was terrified of cloth diapers and Snappis at the time so I used disposables at night until I found a good nighttime dryness solution with cloth (Which I did! I'll share this later in the section called How to Diaper with EC.). The disposables I used were Seventh Generation brand and they were certainly not Huggies...they still helped him feel wet while holding in the leaks.

My newborn bedside set-up (0-4 months)
I co-slept with both of my babies, so I set up a sort of "bumper table" next to the bed – a coffee table with a long pillow on it that comes up higher than our mattress. Next to the pillow on the table was a light with a dimmer switch connected to it (for late-night

visibility during pottying), the BBSP with potty cozy on, and a variety of baskets containing: some cloth wipes to dry him before putting the diaper back on, a changing/peeing on blanket (cloth on one side and plastic on the other), my wipe warmer (glowing with its built-in nightlight) full of scrumptiously warm disposable wipes, disposable and cloth diapers, and a jar of Earth Mama Angel Baby Bottom Balm (invaluable for those red, smelly crevices!). See the Supply List for where I found all these items.

my newborn bedside table set-up for baby #1

This set-up made it so much easier for me to potty my babies at night. Some nights were dry. Some nights were very wet. Some nights they signaled all night. Some nights they were out like a light (probably during a growth spurt, I assumed).

199

My Nighttime Potty Break (somewhere in the 4th-5th month)
Somewhere in the 4th or 5th month I stopped doing nighttime EC for about a week. I was tired, my baby was very tired, and I just stuck him in disposables so we could all get some more sleep. I didn't even offer him the potty when I changed his diaper at night! We did continue our regular daytime EC routines during this nighttime break.

When we both felt better (and after what I thought was a teething/growth spurt combo...subsided), we went back into nighttime EC recharged, with much more success than we'd had before!

My Crawling-Baby Night Pottying Routine (5-8 months)
When my first son turned about 5 months old, he began Army-crawling and his nighttime EC needs coincidentally shifted dramatically. At around 6 months, he would stand up when put on on the mini potty and refuse, vehemently, to sit there and pee, but he wouldn't go back to sleep because he had to pee so badly.

My solution? I started taking him to the bathroom down the hall, every time. I still had a dimmable light on my bedside table, would turn this on low, gently say, "I'm going to take you to potty in the bathroom" to sort of wake him enough to cooperate, would turn on a low light in the bathroom, and would cue him in classic EC position over the sink. Sometimes I quietly sang, sometimes I ran the sink water. Then we'd walk back down the hall, re-diaper, and go peacefully back to sleep. This worked like magic.

My Almost-Walking-Baby Night Pottying Routine (8-9 months)
At 8 months, I trusted my baby's nighttime patterns and let him sleep either naked-bottomed or in his tiny Gerber undies. Every once in a while, I'd wake up about 5-10 minutes in advance of his waking (intuition at play).

When he woke after I woke, I'd offer him the breast. If he went back to sleep, I did, too. If he wriggled, cried out, shifted his head left and right, or crawled, I knew he had to pee and I'd offer it to him. I turned on the dim light by the bed, saying to him, "I'm going to take you to the bathroom now." I carried him gently to the bathroom, turned on a dim light there, put him in the classic EC position over the sink, and said "peepee" or "pssss."

If he resisted it just a little bit, I'd quietly sing "Twinkle, Twinkle" to him and/or run the water. Then we'd return peacefully to bed and I'd either leave him naked-bottomed or put his undies back on.

My Toddler Night Pottying Routine (10-24 months)
My first baby began walking at 9.5 months, shifting our routine in these ways:

He began to protest pottying over the sink at night by crying and arching his back almost every time, sometimes mid-stream!

My solution? Before he got a chance to cry and arch, I nursed him over the sink while cueing him, and he peed while feeding…it took a bit of acrobatics but it mostly worked like a charm!

At 9.5-16 months he began to sleep dry for the first 7-9 of 11 hours of his nighttime sleep. He'd then wake to pee two or three times before waking for the day. It seemed like he could hold it great at night while in deep sleep, but not so much in the morning in his light last hours of sleep.

After many wet beds at around the time when walking began, I returned to using a cloth diaper back-up at night and he began to signal more regularly and stayed drier. During those uncomfortable times of teething and growth spurts, I noticed that he woke up more often and slept a bit lighter, so I gave him homeopathic teething medicine before bed (sometimes throughout the night). This helped his sleep.

At around 17 months he began to hold it for 9-11 hours (the whole night thru at least 5 times a week by 21 months). From 17-21 months he still wore a wool/hemp back-up at night and would wet it maybe once a week. Without it, he'd pee after an hour of sleep. Ah well.

I found that if I nursed him first he'd pee while still sleeping (over the sink, no cue) right after nursing, without fuss. When he'd sleep the whole night thru, I would just take him for his morning pee after snuggling in the morning, unless he signaled that he needed to go right away.

So, at 21 months, we were basically done with nighttime pottying but were still using a back-up ("night-night pants") and switched to just wool soakers at 22 months, just in case.

At 23 months, if he wriggled a whole bunch throughout the night, I offered. If he refused, we went back to bed. No big deal. He'd even call out a signal at night sometimes. If it was for "poop," I did sit him on the mini potty. Otherwise, he still liked being held in-arms.

At 24 months, I weaned him, day and night, and moved him into a sporty wooden race car bed - his Big Boy Bed - and continued the night-night pants for another month or two.

Then, as it was winter and he hated using a blanket, I dressed him naked in fleece footed pajamas for nighttime sleep. He peed in those once and then rarely again thereafter. It felt gross, I'd assume, and he just got old enough (and capable enough) to hold it or wake me up to pee from that age onward. Without the night-night pants, he held it much better from there on out.

Again, this was our journey. Yours will likely differ. Enjoy your unique experience!

SOME THINGS TO REMEMBER

- Good instruction & creative options make nighttime EC less scary
- An easy-access bedside setup of gear helps
- Using cloth diapers or modified disposables may help you complete nighttime dryness sooner
- Nighttime EC can shift from night to night...remain flexible and open
- Nighttime EC helps Daytime EC, and vice versa
- Nighttime EC is good for Part-timers and Working Parents

- Some babies get better sleep if they are pottied intermittently at night, others don't (You will/won't, too.)
- When you're all really tired...get some rest. Nap in the day with baby.
- Parenting at night is as important as in the daytime...be gentle, communicative, and wise about your activities!

And remember...only do Nighttime EC if everyone in the family gets more restful sleep. Otherwise, night dryness usually comes naturally, in time, as a byproduct of daytime dryness.

PART-TIME EC

EC FOR WORKING PARENTS (& OTHER PART-TIMERS)

Another topic that concerns ECing families is how to continue EC when the parents go back to work...or decide they just want to do EC part-time.

This special section is for Working Parents...and it is also for those families who, although with their baby full-time, choose to EC part-time based on their family lifestyle choices.

TIPS FOR MAINTAINING A PART-TIME EC PRACTICE

If you have already begun ECing your child and have to return to work outside of the home, are starting EC while already working outside the home, or if you are simply choosing to maintain your EC practice part-time, there are a few routes you can take to help your baby continue this learning while avoiding confusion and interruption.

PRACTICE EC CONSISTENTLY DURING TIMES AT HOME / SPECIFIC TIMES

You can simply practice EC during those times when you are at home with your baby, or during specific times that suit your family's lifestyle. These times can include mornings, evenings, nights, and/or weekends.

Besides helping your baby stay sensitive to his awareness of and ability to communicate about elimination, your other goal is to expose your baby to the potty regularly so that it's familiar and comfortable (instead of suddenly introducing it at a much later age).

SHOOT FOR THE EASY CATCHES

If you can potty your baby upon waking, you're certain to catch a pee. Also, pottytunities during diaper changes are pretty reliable. See the end of this section for a sample schedule that includes a list of good pottytunities for the working or part-time ECer.

REGULARLY GIVE DIAPER-FREE TIME

Give your baby diaper-free time as often as you are comfortable and able. But remember: do it responsibly. Once you've got the necessary info, use undies, trainers, or just pants so your baby doesn't get used to peeing on the floor.

If you can do a half hour or more daily, that's recommended. If not, shoot for at least once per week. A little diaper-free time before the evening bath is always nice!

CONSIDER CO-SLEEPING AT NIGHT

Many working ECers find success at staying in touch with baby's signals and timing needs by co-sleeping. If you co-sleep, you will increase your connection and familiarity with your baby, and will be physically able to sense her signals and needs and thus respond more quickly, sending you both back to sleep more quickly.

Co-sleeping can be done in a safe manner and in an arrangement that helps the whole family get more sleep than if the baby sleeps in a crib, alone. Do whatever gives your family the most sleep and allows you to remain more closely and intuitively connected with your baby.

Babies need to discharge pent-up energy that they generate throughout the day and the top two ways to help them do this (and produce a happier, more serene baby) are by co-sleeping and babywearing. Not only do these activities deepen your intuition and results around EC, but they also help you both feel happier & more connected!

PRACTICE NIGHTTIME EC

On the note of co-sleeping, you might also consider ramping up your nighttime EC practice in lieu of your daytime. Nighttime EC is easier and less disruptive to the whole family if you co-sleep, but has been successfully done without co-sleeping.

It is true that some people become exhausted by practicing nighttime EC. It's also true that some people get more sleep because baby is more comfortable (having an empty bladder)…it just depends. Doing nighttime EC can positively influence any effort at daytime EC. It can also prevent bedwetting in later years. Refer to the section in this book on Nighttime EC to learn more. Give it a try and see what happens.

WEAR YOUR BABY MORE OFTEN

During those times when you are home, skip the stroller and carry your baby in a sling or other type of baby carrier. As with co-sleeping, being physically closer to your baby via wearing her attunes you to her signals and natural timing around pottying (and many other things!). It also deepens your connection during the precious moments you spend together when you're not at work.

As I said in the co-sleeping section above, babies need to discharge pent-up energy that they generate throughout the day and the top two ways to help them do this (and produce a happier, more serene baby) are by co-sleeping and babywearing. Not only do these activities deepen your intuition and results around EC, but they also help you both feel happier & more connected!

Use Cloth Diapers (or Modified Disposables) at Least Part-time

If you are unable to do EC full-time (whether you are away at work or simply choosing to EC part-time), try switching to cloth diapers at least part-time. While you are with your baby, put her in a cloth diaper held in place by a belt or elastic band (without a plastic cover over it – think "Sumo Wrestler").

Do this so you can immediately feel when your baby is wet and either offer a pottytunity to see if there's more or simply change the diaper. Your baby needs to remain accustomed to dryness, so, if you are able to, do this as often as possible.

You will also remain in touch with your baby's Natural Timing if you know immediately when she's wet, and her Signals (as they evolve) will also remain more clear and consistent.

Disposable diapers alone will not help you achieve these goals…however, there is a way to modify their use by adding a cut-up piece of a washcloth (see How to Diaper with EC for how to do both the cloth sumo-style & the disposable modification).

Caregivers & EC

If you are in a situation where you must hire a caregiver (such as a nanny) or bring your child to daycare while you work (or do other things), try to find a caregiver who will participate with ECing your child to some extent.

During your initial interview, ask your caregiver if s/he has had any experience with EC. Many caregivers who are natives of other countries may have been exposed to some form of EC in their homeland's culture but may not apply this to your baby <u>unless you ask</u>. If you are interviewing a foreign native, inquire about the potty learning activities used in their homeland. You may be surprised at what you discover!

If you are interviewing someone who isn't familiar with EC, ask if s/he would be willing to learn EC and help your baby go when she signals. Download, print, and fill out my special guide titled **EC**

Guide for Caregivers and give it to your caregiver (available in the Readers' Area).

This guide will introduce your caregiver to how to cue, what your baby's signals are, and what her preferred positions are. Request s/he read and study it. Demonstrate for him/her how you EC your baby.

Daycares may be a little more of a challenge, but give it a shot. Perhaps your daycare attendant could offer your baby a pottytunity during the time when the toddlers and other young children take a potty break. You can also ask them to change baby's diaper every hour, on the hour, so she'll stay more dry (download and print my document called **A Letter to the Daycare** and give it to the supervising attendant - available in the Readers' Area).

Just knowing that your baby sometimes cries to go potty will help your caregiver, daycare or otherwise, have an easier time caring for your child.

IF YOU ARE UNABLE TO FIND AN EC-WILLING CAREGIVER:

1. Do your best to keep your child's sensitivity alive during the times you are with him by following the advice above.
2. Ask your caregiver to change your baby's wet diapers OFTEN. You can mention that you've had problems with diaper rash in the past and the best way to avoid it is to change her every hour (or any time increment of your choice).
3. Request that a daycare attendant bring your baby to the potty when other older children are given a potty break. Show him/her how to potty your baby with what equipment they've got.
4. Give the daycare attendant a letter (A Letter to the Daycare) to help you request #2 & #3 in a more formal way.
5. Re-approach the subject with your caregiver at a later date and see if s/he has become open to it (especially if the baby regularly gets fussy when she wants to pee and the caregiver wants her to be less fussy while in his/her care!)

6. Many babies quickly learn that their parent will potty them when they drop them off/pick them up, but the caregiver will not, and it doesn't confuse them.
7. Follow the example below to give your baby a prime number of pottytunities before and after dropping him off for care.

EXAMPLE: "A DAY IN THE LIFE OF A WORKING EC PARENT"

Here's an illustration of how and when to potty your baby before and after work, taking advantage of various Pottytunities (based on both your baby's Natural Timing and other common times [Generic Timing]).

1. Offer a pottytunity immediately upon waking first thing in the morning, and thereafter as frequently as you think your baby might have to potty until you have to go to work. (Observe during diaper-free time on weekends to learn how often your baby usually has to go in the mornings.)
2. Before leaving for daycare, offer a pottytunity.
3. At daycare when you drop your baby off, offer a final pottytunity inside (bring a potty with you or use their toilet

or sink). You can mention to your baby that she may have to pee in her diaper during the day, but that Mommy/Daddy has asked the attendant to change her often.

4. When you pick baby up from daycare, offer a pottytunity while you're inside.

5. When you get out of the car at home, offer a pottytunity.

6. Put her in a cloth diaper held in place with a diaper belt or elastic band once you get home (or use tiny underwear or training pants). Notice when she's wet and change her immediately. If/when she signals, offer her pottytunities based on her needs. (You can also use a modified disposable – see How to Diaper with EC).

7. Offer pottytunities at every diaper change.

8. Offer at least 1/2 hour of diaper-free time before her evening bath or after dinner. If she begins to pee on the floor without signaling (and is a mobile baby), softly, gently transport her to the potty and say "pee in the potty." If she's younger and this happens, just cue along with her.

The key here is for baby to loosen her dependence upon diapers via diaper-free time. Remember that this includes time spent in underwear, trainers, or just pants.

Diaper-free time (at least once per week) is essential. If she does signal, take her to the proper place and mention "You went peepee in the potty/sink/bathroom. That's where peepee goes." Or say nothing! And remember...do diaper-free time responsibly.

9. Offer a final pottytunity prior to going to bed.

10. On the weekends, offer pottytunities upon waking from naps.

11. If you are up to it, learn how to Nighttime EC and try co-sleeping to enhance the practice as a whole. See the section on Nighttime EC for more.

12. Keep baby in EC-friendly clothing during the times you choose to EC (see the Supply List).

As you can see by this example, it is possible to do a lot of EC if you choose to practice it part-time or if you must return to work!

DIAPERS + DIAPER-FREE TIME

INTRODUCTION

This section contains everything regarding using diapers as a back-up...without teaching your baby to pee on the floor.

The main areas of focus are three:

1. How to Diaper with EC
2. Do I Have to Do Away with Diapers?
3. Doing Regular Diaper-free Time, Responsibly

Pretty much everything you'll ever need to know about using diapers as tools in your EC practice will be covered in this section.

How to Diaper with EC

If you want to EC with a diaper back-up, this section demystifies simple cloth diapering options & EC-friendly disposable diapering options.

Like many moms, I was baffled by cloth diapers in the beginning. I really wanted to use them because I believed that keeping my baby in cloth would encourage him out of diapers sooner (not to mention I felt guilty landfilling disposables!!).

But I couldn't get them to fit correctly on my little newborn boy. I watched video after video and tried so hard, but ended up pausing my cloth diaper service & using disposables as a back-up until I could figure it all out!

Since then, I've used both cloth & disposables, in many different ways, throughout our EC journey. I now use cloth 95% of my diapering back-up time.

What have I learned? First of all, there is not much to fear around cloth diapering...in fact, you can do it with very little expense or expertise. I also learned that choosing disposables will not destroy your EC practice if you use them responsibly.

In this section I equip you with 4 ways to diaper your baby for easy & inexpensive ECing.

You will learn:
- basic cloth diapering vocabulary
- 2 methods of cloth diapering, simplified for EC
- how to pre-wash & wash cloth diapers at home
- 2 disposable diapering options: 1) with an insert to maintain sensitivity, and 2) without getting baby used to wetness or getting diaper rash

Let's get started!

CLOTH DIAPERING VOCABULARY

Remember that all of the items you might possibly need to diaper with EC are found in the Supply List toward the end of this book. Here's a list of general cloth diapering vocab!

Prefold - a cloth diaper that has a thicker center area and two thinner outer areas. Usually made of 100% cotton, some are made of uber-absorbent hemp or a combination of these and other fibers. Prefolds come in various sizes based on age & weight, however, they can be used more creatively than prescribed. AKA "Trifold," "Diaper," "Cloth Diaper"

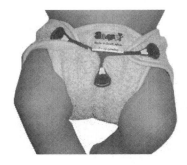

Snappi - a safer mechanism for holding a prefold together without having to use a diaper pin. They hold a prefold in place on your baby (then you top that with a cover, or not). However, I don't recommend these for EC use...they become an obstacle.

216

Diaper Cover - a water-resistant outer cover that helps contain pee and poo when the prefold becomes soiled. The cover usually wraps around the prefold/snappi combo, but I use it just over a folded prefold in the Quick EC Diaper method below. Made of wool, cotton, polyester, or a blend, with or without a plastic inner liner. AKA "Diaper Shell"

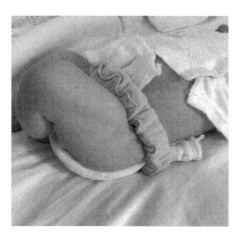

Diaper Belt - an elasticized band wrapped in a moisture-resistant cloth outer covering (such as wool or fleece) which holds a prefold in place, Sumo Wrestler style. The belt stays on the baby's waist between changes. AKA "Prefold Belt"

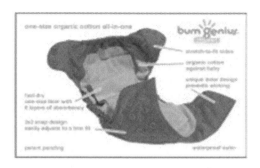

Cloth Diapering System or AIO - AKA "All In One Diaper," this basically means that somebody created a cloth diapering 'system' that can be conveniently & easily used, laundered, and understood. Funny, because I have a hard time wrapping my mind around them!

You don't need to invest in an AIO system for EC, although many people do and love them. You might use the covers (or "shells") alone, as per the Quick EC Diaper method, below. I've never bought the "kits," just the covers.

2 CLOTH DIAPERING METHODS

Using cloth diapers does not have to be complex or expensive. Try these two quick, easy, inexpensive methods:

1) Quick EC Diaper

I developed this method based on what I had on-hand and my need to have a simple diaper-back-up system. Basically, the Quick EC Diaper is a folded-over cloth prefold in a diaper cover.

The diaper cover serves to keep the prefold in place and keeps a big miss contained better than method #2, below, due to snug leg gussets in the covers.

The Quick EC Diaper, Step-by-Step
My Daytime Set-up
(Grovia Cover w/100% Cotton Prefold)

Lay your diaper cover out flat...

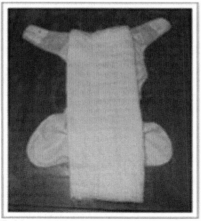

Fold a prefold diaper lengthwise in half,

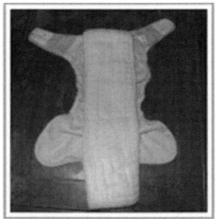

*or thirds...and lay this inside a cloth diaper cover.
Line up the top of the folded prefold with the top of the back of the cover.
Do not pin, clip, nor secure the cloth diaper onto baby with a Snappi...
simply lay it in the cover.*

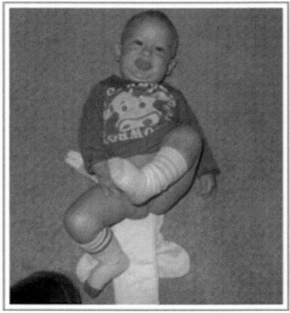

*Lay your baby on top of the diaper, lining up the top seam of the back of the
diaper to belly-button-height.*

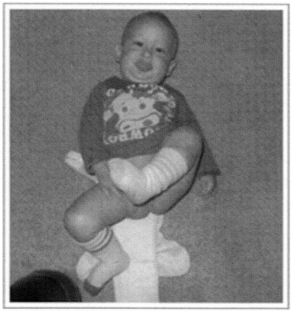

Fasten the diaper cover (with prefold laying in it) on your baby & you're done.

The Quick EC Diaper, Step-by-Step
My Nighttime Set-up
(Imse Vimse Wool Cover w/Hemp/Cotton Prefold)

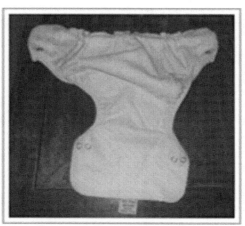

Lay your diaper cover out flat....

Fold your hemp/cotton prefold diaper lengthwise in thirds... and lay this inside a cloth diaper cover. Line up the top of the folded prefold with the top of the back of the cover.

Do not pin, clip, nor secure the cloth diaper onto baby with a Snappi... simply lay it in the cover.

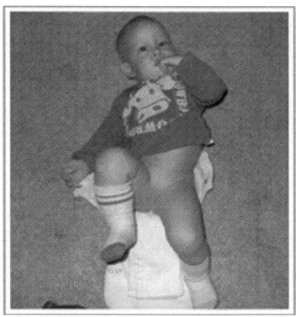

Lay your baby on top of the diaper, lining up the top seam of the back of the diaper to belly-button-height.

222

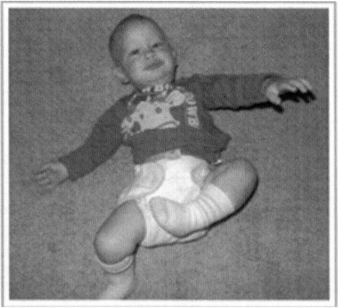

Fasten the diaper cover (with prefold laying in it) on your baby & you're done.

Materials: For daytime, use a cotton prefold in a cloth diaper cover of your choice. For nighttime use the same...OR...if you're finding you need more absorbency, day or night, use a hemp/cotton blend prefold in a wool diaper cover to minimize leaks, or a hemp/cotton blend prefold in a cotton diaper cover if your baby doesn't need as much protection.

Don't want to spend time figuring out which covers & prefolds to buy? See the Supply List for my simple recommendations of what you'll need to diaper in this way.

Sizing: Use a prefold size that lays in the diaper cover exactly and doesn't stick out the end, either direction, once affixed to your baby. For this, newborn-sized prefolds work for a VERY long time on most babies. Upgrade if you ever find it necessary. We've used newborn-sized prefolds for 11 months straight in this manner, with a diaper cover that grows with the baby (Grovia).

Start-up Costs:
Day
$1.50 x 20 cotton prefolds = $30*
4 cloth diaper covers x $17 = $68

Night
$7 x 6 hemp/cotton prefolds = $42
1 wool diaper cover x $30 = $30
Total Cost = $170

with a newborn, I recommend buying 40 prefolds to start (add $30 to total), or just using a diaper service for the first 2 months.

Considering most cloth diapering systems cost upwards of $300-400, this is method can be used at a great savings.

2) Sumo-Style Diaper
For a super-simple diaper-back-up method, use a diaper belt, AKA prefold belt, holding a prefold diaper in place.

To instantly tell when your baby's wet, day or night, use this method.

Use it if you're not able to do diaper-free time, or for nighttime if you want a simple diaper changing option.

Sumo-style Diaper, Step-by-Step
(w/Cotton Prefold)

Place the diaper belt on the baby's waist.
Fold a prefold cloth diaper in half or thirds and place between baby's legs.

Pull either end into the diaper belt on the front and back of baby's waist, holding the diaper into place with a bit hanging out of each side.

front view

back view

Then you can easily pull the diaper off the baby, while leaving the diaper belt on her waist!

226

Materials: In general, use 100% cotton prefolds. You can also use the more absorbent hemp/cotton prefolds at night if you need an extra boost. Get (or make) a diaper belt made of a water-repellent material, such as wool, cotton flannel, or fleece.

Sizing: As opposed to the Quick EC Diaper method, for the Sumo-style you'll want the prefold to stick out of the ends of the diaper belt. This keeps it in place.

For newborns, use preemie or newborn-sized prefolds. For larger babies, use newborn, infant or toddler-sized (depending on your baby's size) so the diaper will fit around your baby and through the belt (front and back).

Start-up Costs:
1 diaper belt = $8

Day
$1.50 x 20 cotton prefolds = $30*

Night
$7 x 6 hemp/cotton prefolds = $42
Total Cost = $80

with a newborn, I recommend buying 40 prefolds to start (add $30 to total), or just using a diaper service for the first 2 months.

The sumo-style method of back-up diapering can also save a tremendous amount of money compared to the cost of most cloth diapering systems ($300-400).

Did you know?
Most Americans spend an average of **$3,000** on disposable diapers over the diaper-wearing years (an average of 3 years)!

HOW TO PRE-WASH & WASH CLOTH DIAPERS AT HOME

With a peed-in diaper just throw it in the wash. You could also rinse with warm water and hang dry to use a few times prior to laundering.

When you have a poopy diaper to contend with (which isn't usual, but *does* happen), this is how to pre-wash & wash:

1. Get the poo off the prefold. I try to get the poo into the toilet. If it's breastmilk-only poo, it can go down the sink. If it's solid, I wipe it off with a piece of toilet paper or try to gently shake it off. Solid poo is actually kind of easy to get into the toilet. Liquid poo…go for the sink. If you have a bidet, use it to spray the poo off. You can find some DIY bidet solutions for cloth diapering by searching online, but to keep it simple, I just wipe or shake into the toilet.
2. Run water over the whole prefold. I use hot water, others recommend cold. Your choice.
3. Squirt some hand soap (or any time of soap) onto the prefold where the mess is. You may have to squirt a few areas.
4. Hold the prefold in your left hand and use your right hand to rub the prefold against itself, using the heel of your left hand as the 'scrubbing board.' Scrub together until the stain mostly comes out, adding more soap when necessary.
5. Rinse the prefold with water, wring out, and hang dry.
6. Do the same with your diaper cover…dump any solids, get wet, squirt on some hand soap, scrub, rinse, and hang dry.
7. Throw both prefold and diaper cover into the laundry at any point thereafter.
8. I recommend washing any baby clothing, including diapers, in a natural laundry detergent, such as Seventh Generation's Free & Clear. This reduces the chance of diaper rash!

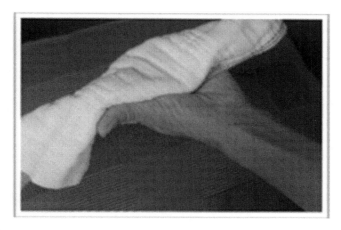

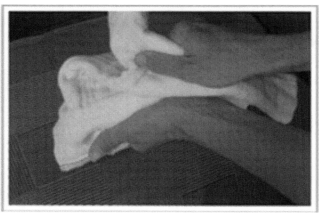

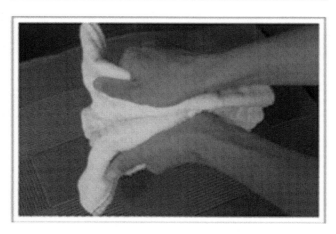

CONSIDER HIRING A CLOTH DIAPER SERVICE

To ease my anxiety of having a new baby with tons of new responsibilities, I asked a relative to gift me with a cloth diaper service for the first two months. I was able to skip the wash-them-myself stage and learn to use cloth the way I wanted to. In the San Francisco Bay Area, TinyTots is the best for their amazing customer service and fair prices.

2 DISPOSABLE DIAPER OPTIONS

You can EC with disposable diapers. I did for the first two months with my first as I unraveled the mystery of how to use cloth diapers, and occasionally over the first five months (such as while traveling or driving long distances). I've used them much longer with subsequent babies and had great results.

We like seeing how long we can use "this one dry disposable diaper" throughout a day. Re-use disposables so long as they are dry!

You can use disposables "responsibly" for optimum-EC results by doing the following:

1) Add A Cloth Insert

If you want to continue to use disposable diapers but want your baby to remain sensitive to wetness, get some old wash cloths, cut them into thirds, and drop one of the strips into the disposable diaper. That way you can either wash the strips or chuck 'em with the diapers, but it gives some feedback to the child and doesn't involve spending the money to switch to cloth diapers.

Buy used washcloths at the thrift store or request free ones by posting a listing on Craigslist.

230

2) Change Diaper Frequently

If you just want the simple route of using disposables but want to make them EC-friendly, try this:

Change your baby frequently and offer pottytunities upon each changing. You will likely find that the diaper is still dry. See how long you can use this one dry disposable diaper…make it a game.

Resist the implied "convenience" of disposable diapers. Do not let your baby sit in a wet diaper for too long. Always dry the baby's skin after using a wet-wipe to avoid diaper rash.

See my Supply List for my disposable diaper brand recommendation and for a little-known way to save 15-20% off in-store prices. Gotta love a bargain…

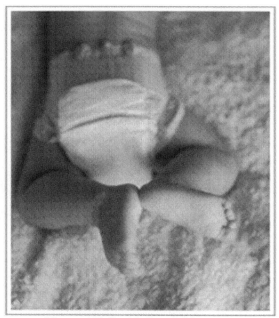

You can EC with disposables, too….

Do I Have to Do Away with Diapers?

The phrase diaper-free actually means "free from an exclusive reliance on diapers." It does not imply that you must EC without diapers, although some do. Most folks choose to EC with a diaper back-up, or some variation in between.

Parents do EC within a wide spectrum of diaper usage – from none to all the way! Here is a visual to help you see the array of options you can choose from – or create your own.

The Continuum of Diaper Usage in EC

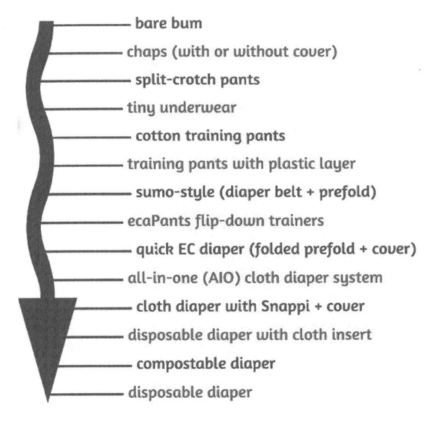

- bare bum
- chaps (with or without cover)
- split-crotch pants
- tiny underwear
- cotton training pants
- training pants with plastic layer
- sumo-style (diaper belt + prefold)
- ecaPants flip-down trainers
- quick EC diaper (folded prefold + cover)
- all-in-one (AIO) cloth diaper system
- cloth diaper with Snappi + cover
- disposable diaper with cloth insert
- compostable diaper
- disposable diaper

Using the back-up as a "tool"

Something that might help you choose which method to select is the idea that the diaper, training pants, or underwear should be seen and used as a "tool." This tool will ideally keep misses and messes contained while your baby learns and matures, will help you EC without stress, will aid you in easy on's and off's, and will encourage your baby to signal most.

Choose your tool wisely, and allow for it to morph as you and your baby's needs evolve. See my Supply List to find all the great stuff I've listed above.

WHEN TO DITCH THE DIAPERS

You'll someday make the decision to stop using diapers altogether. For example, a reader in India reports: "babies will wear some sort of thin cloth diaper there until they can be counted on to reliably signal [or timing/intuition is reliable] that they have to go." You will know when.

When you do ditch 'em, you can use training pants if *you* need extra protection for some reason (like the new white carpet, or your nerves, or your MIL's upcoming visit). Or, you can move directly to underwear or commando (pants only). Some parents find success with this because it's an actual "shift" from diapers to not diapers.

An example: we went from diapers to Gerber training pants [at 9 months] to undies/commando [at 15 months]...which was great for us because of the carpet! Remember – pick your best "tool."

But you can do it anytime! (And you can experiment with what sort of clothing/back-up you'd like to move into.) Just don't ditch them in order to gain "supremo EC status" or something! It's not a contest. Heed the Indian gal's advice.

You might also choose to only use them on outings, only while at Grandma's house, or only as a tool during a re-set.

As for nighttime and naps, you may continue using diapers as a back-up for longer than daytime (most parents do, although some just use undies and a soaker pad underneath...your choice – just be aware of what you're teaching here). Using a cloth nighttime back-up is a good idea if you all need to sleep better, and if your babe simply communicates this way better. I used one with my son for 24 months and 99% of the time it was dry in the morning.

Just keep communicating. And know that most kiddos naturally become dry at night after daytime dryness becomes regular. Use the sleepy-time back-up until you know it keeps coming up dry, or until you feel like it's time to ditch the dipes the whole 24/7.

USING THE DIAPER DURING A RE-SET

You may get to the end of your rope and need a way to "re-set" your EC practice...to get your kiddo to start signaling again...to stop the potty-centered tone that's gone rampant in the house...to get a sanity-saving break...to focus on other things!

Re-setting can be amazing for you both.

Remember: Using a diaper as a "tool" is different than just diapering her up and not communicating about it anymore!

To do a re-set by re-diapering for a short period, mark your calendar for 2 weeks and use a diaper back-up as a "re-set," 24/7. First, tell your kiddo you're using diapers again for 2 weeks because he's still learning, and that you want him to tell you when he needs to go. He'll understand.

If she signals strongly, or you see the nonverbal signals clearly, go ahead and potty your baby (silently) but do not make it the focus of your day. (It should never be the focus of your day, anyway!)

As you further let go, you will all relax...things will shift...and the diaper-as-tool thing will finally make sense. Just keep it to simple communicating if you choose to do a re-set. Brief phrases. (And swallow your pride. Again, this is not about being the first Mom or Dad on the block whose infant is out of diapers!)

PS – I did a re-set at 13 months and it's the best thing I EVER did. Seriously.

DOING REGULAR DIAPER-FREE TIME, *RESPONSIBLY*

I added this section because recent trends show that overdoing naked diaper-free time can actually hinder the EC process, teaching a child to pee on the floor. Read on....

THE BOTTOM LINE

IF your baby signals best while naked and you don't have a peeing-on-the-floor problem, then do naked time as much as you want!

If your baby doesn't signal when naked, and there is pee everywhere, then you're better off limiting naked time.

THE IMPORTANCE OF DIAPER-FREE TIME

Although diapers are commonly used as a back-up, after you're finished with Part 1, Step 1, and diaper-free observation time has served its purpose, you may choose to continue giving your baby some diaper-free time every day or week.

1/2 hour per day is common, and before bathtime is popular. The most important thing here is to do any naked diaper-free time *responsibly*. Here's how....

DECIDING WHETHER TO CONTINUE OFFERING DIAPER-FREE TIME

Once naked or modified diaper-free observation time has served its purpose (to inform you of your baby's signals and natural timing, and to inform your baby of what her own elimination feels like, which is what the whole "Part 1, Step 1" was all about), you can decide whether you want to keep doing regular diaper-free time or not, naked or not.

The key here is that diaper-free time can mean naked or without diapers (in clothing or undies or whatnot).

You will know when you are done with the diapers. You will know when naked time will benefit. You will know when it's time for underwear…or when it's time to strike a middle ground. If you don't, visit me in our Private Support Group and we'll have a little chat. No worries!

In general, lots of folks start doing away with diapers when their babies resist them more than not, or even begin to prefer other things like underwear. This can begin around pre-walking or 9 months. Usually by around 14 months parents start to look at permanently ditching daytime diapers. We did it at 9 months and it was a lot of pants/undies laundry for a few months…but it felt right for our son.

But let's take a look at the main culprit here: whether and how to do **NAKED TIME** or not. Because that's the real point of this section!

WHEN *NAKED* TIME BECOMES COUNTER-PRODUCTIVE

When naked, no one needs to signal, now do they?! **Naked** time (observation or regular) can become counter-productive when:
- you already know his signals
- you already know his current natural timing
- and *baby* is already aware of what's going on down there.

If you've got all this going for ya, naked observation time may have already served its purpose. Any naked time beyond this and you could essentially be teaching him to pee on the floor (depending on how you handle things). In EC terms, if you continue to give naked time when it's become counter-productive, you are just being lazy. Sorry.

But it's no different than using a diaper all the time, teaching baby "pee in here." Too much naked time without communication or action or any boundaries will result in teaching "pee wherever."

It could be time to add in some 'resistance' (think: opposite poles of a magnet): **clothing**, since soiling his clothing will eventually not feel socially/physically/emotionally cool, clothing can and may become your new "diaper-free time." Remember…"Diaper-free" means free from exclusive dependence upon diapers. It doesn't mean having a naked baby or toddler running around peeing all over your floor 24/7.

236

Once observation is complete, you'll want to know how to continue diaper-free and/or naked time...responsibly. First let's state the obvious.

HOW TO CONTINUE DIAPER-FREE TIME, *NOT NAKED*

Pick a time of day and a desired location to do some time with underwear or just pants (commando) as your "back-up." Training pants often feel like a diaper, but see how your baby responds. Increase this non-diaper time over the weeks and before you know it you will be done with dipes. Now let's cover how to continue naked time....

SOME REASONS TO <u>NOT</u> KEEP DOING *NAKED* TIME

First of all, your baby could stop signaling as strongly, or at all. Which makes sense. **Why signal if I'm already naked?!!**

Next, your baby might learn that peeing on the floor, or on the cloth he's laying on, is okay. Which it's not, really...right? Right.

Lastly, we wear clothing in our society, so your baby will also need to learn how to wear clothing and not soil it.

REASONS TO <u>KEEP</u> DOING *NAKED* TIME

If you are starting with a more mobile baby (5 months+, and especially 12 months+), you may decide to spend some additional time naked to reinforce the cause & effect rule. If you just like having a naked baby bum around, no matter the baby's age, you might want to do more nakey time too.

If you have a baby who doesn't pee on the floor when naked, go for it ya'll! If baby signals *better when naked*, awesome. Do it. Also, if you struggle with diaper rash, naked time is one of the only things that helps. So you'd want to do it then, too.

In any case, just see #3, below, to learn how to modify it with an older baby so you don't teach her to pee on the floor (again, a common problem faced by some ECers).

HOW TO *MODIFY NAKED TIME* AFTER ITS PURPOSE IS SERVED...AND WHEN BABY BECOMES MOBILE

Okay, so you've gathered your info (signals/timing/awareness), cleared up the diaper rash, want to continue having a naked feral child, whatever. Your child is becoming more mobile by the day...and her brain is building permanent pathways on how to do stuff.

Let's modify naked time to place some building blocks for eventual potty independence into your EC practice:

1. Put your babe in clothing (unless doing purposeful naked time – see #3): this could be trainers, tiny underwear, or elastic-topped pants that are easy to remove. Experiment to see which clothing your baby signals most in/responds best to...and what set-up causes you to retain the most sanity.

2. When you're done using day-time diapers, take the plunge and use trainers, tiny underwear, or go commando with pants only. Many parents do this at 9+ months. You might have some laundry, but I want you to know that this counts as "diaper-free time." Yay!

3. Modeling "to the potty" During Naked Time (Mobile Babies) – When your baby has hit 9 months or so (when the ability to consistently hold a short-term memory kicks in, and when baby becomes more mobile), it's time to demonstrate moving to the potty during naked diaper-free time.

Bottom Line: You don't want to teach your mobile baby that it's okay to pee on the floor. Right? Right.

So, as soon as naked diaper-free time as served it purpose (signals/timing/awareness) **and** the [approximate] 9 month mark has been reached, **when** you see your baby peeing or pooing during naked diaper-free time say "wait" or "potty" and quietly, gently, move her to the potty and sit her on it. If you only catch a drop, that's fine.

Do not panic, do not become gruff, excited, or angry. Just matter-of-factly guide her by bringing her to the potty. Do not bring the

238

potty to her. Do not say much. In fact, if you want to say something that will model for her what to say to you when she needs to go in the future, say "I need to peepee Mama/Papa" while you airlift her. Again, your goal here is to model what it's like to take herself to the potty.

Note: If she is playing with something when she starts to pee, bring the toy or book with her. This will prevent potential meltdown.

If you get resistance, hold her for a sec before putting her down. Or check your own relaxation level. Deep breath.

If you don't feel like doing this transporting stuff, then don't do naked diaper-free time that often, or exclude it from your practice by using underwear or training pants at all times. (Again, this also qualifies as "diaper-free time"!)

Okay! So, keep #3 in mind for older babies, or for when your newborn is older.

Where the pee goes

THE BUILDING BLOCKS OF POTTY INDEPENDENCE

STEPS TO POTTY INDEPENDENCE + GRADUATION

This section will help you do what no other EC resource will: it gives you the basic building blocks of completing EC with your little one. It is also optional...you can do EC without this if you want. And for those who have been asking for this, here you go....

I believe that every child, of the appropriate developmental stage and capability, deserves to feel the mastery of completing a process. With pottying, this involves mastery over a process regarding your child's very own body. This is huge! First let's clear up how we ECers got here.

THE HISTORY OF "DON'T FOCUS ON COMPLETION"

It totally makes sense why ECers shy away from focus on completion. It creates PRESSURE. Pressure does not equal EC. EC is gentle, communicative, and follows your baby's innate rhythms. Completion seems counter to all of this go-with-the-flow kinda stuff. I agree, and I also disagree.

Completion should <u>not</u> be on the forefront of your mind when you are beginning EC. It will inevitably pressure the whole situation. It will become more about being the first child out of diapers, less about EC. Competitive Parenting is not healthy. It just isn't.

HOWEVER...completion <u>IS</u> part of the EC process. Completion is part of EVERY process!

"Don't Focus on Completion" is akin to saying "Wait til they're ready." It sounds good on the surface but, deeper down, it just doesn't hold up. About 1 in 500 kids tell a parent they are ready to be potty trained. And, I'd assume the same percentage of ECed kids just naturally complete with zero taught skills or guidance of any sort, on their own.

We teach the alphabet. We begin this process holding the desire for our child to eventually master reading and writing, but we do not let

242

it pressure the process. We teach the skill of the alphabet and then continue to build on that, teaching other skills, until reading is eventually mastered.

It's no different to teach our children the "building blocks" of pottying so that they can one day do it themselves. And it doesn't need to involve coercion, pressure, or rewards. Just developmentally-appropriate teaching.

If you prefer to do purist EC, I'll support ya. Simply omit this section. Don't teach. Just know that, as it stood before this book revision, most parents of ECed children have had to either figure out their own way of completing the process, feeling intuitively that there must be an end to it, or have let it drag on too long, not knowing what else to do.

EC did not (for them) prepare their children for potty independence because it lacked certain taught skills. If you decide that you want to teach your child some things that will naturally complement the inevitable end to this process, read on....

OTHER CULTURES COMPLETE

I once read that tribal Mamas would "shoo" their babies out of the house if they had a miss on the floor when they were beyond the age of "knowing better." So, there is an understanding between mother and child that basically says, "Hey, you know the drill. Take care of it yourself, the way you learned that we all do it."

It's not done in a harsh way, this "shooing." It's actually just socialization, and since we don't pee everywhere, and we wear clothes, your child also gets to be socialized! The *way* you do it is what makes it EC, and not conventional toilet training.

You rooted your EC practice in listening to your child's signals and then responding by helping her do what she couldn't yet do herself. This is Communication.

Taking it to the next step, it is now your job to teach/model/demonstrate how she can start doing it herself. I fondly call it "Passing the Baton." It happens in little stages, when you know a piece is missing, and it helps to empower the little person who is grasping for things she can "do myself."

It is not done with force or coercion. It is just a little "on-the-job training"...because, yes, babies are born wanting to potty hygienically, but they aren't born knowing how to pull down their pants, sit on a foreign object like a potty (and stay there), or how to state their need in a form that you clearly understand (like a phrase!). Passing the Baton can be fun, rewarding, and a feeling of mastery will warm you both.

PERMISSION TO TEACH

Before we get into how to pass said baton, I'd like to give you permission to teach your child. Might sound silly, but in our current breeding generations we have a block about this. Which sometimes results in feral mutant tyrant children.

We've, as the natural, gentle parenting generations, gone from our parents' strict authoritarian styles to some which are completely permissive. As Dr. Sears shared in his books on Attachment Parenting, especially The Discipline Book, both of those styles aren't gonna work. Somewhere in between we can take charge and be gentle at the same time.

Somewhere along the way, "teaching" has become a questionable practice. "Training" has been black listed. Understandably!

In this book I share with you that "EC is not 'training' your baby. EC is listening to the signals your baby is already giving and helping her meet her instinctual needs for cleanliness and dryness." And this is true. This is how it begins, anyway.

But there *does* come a time for teaching (like I said, you can consider it on-the-job training, if you wish!). So, I hereby give you permission to teach. To enable. To facilitate. To demonstrate. To model. Whatever you want to call it. And I give you permission to do it at the appropriate developmental phase, no earlier.

And I give you permission to not overdo it, not hyperfocus on it, to teach, leave space for absorption (silence, time, space), and be balanced in your teaching. I do not give you permission to nag, criticize, helicopter, hover, hound, or "make crazy" your child…nor to expect more of them than is psychologically, physically, emotionally, mentally, or physiologically possible at any particular age.

EC CAN DRAG ON…

The field of Elimination Communication already gets mixed reviews in the media. When EC drags on in an unhealthy way, well beyond the age where a toddler is capable of doing it himself, this inadvertently gives EC a bad rap.

It's kinda like allowing a child to poop in a diaper for 4 years. Allowing a kid to "pee anywhere" for 4 years is very similar, idn't it?

It's not the fault of the parent, but the lack of relevant information on completion and the fuzzy philosophical background of EC which cause the negative PR. Basically, it makes EC look bad…and further shakes our personal confidence in the practice.

The cool thing is that we can prevent EC from dragging on in an unhealthy way. Although parenting toddlers can be difficult and bewildering at times (I feel that!), they are also begging for mastery. It is developmentally necessary for things to be mastered. So we can help!

WHY MASTERY IS SO ESSENTIAL FOR TODDLERS

Toddlers throw fits. They make ridiculous (to us) demands. They have tantrums. Ok, maybe yours doesn't, but mine does. Part of why they throw a fit is this: they want to do it themselves but can't quite do it just yet. And that's deeply frustrating for them.

By teaching some things, like the building blocks I'm about to share with you, you can lessen your toddler's frustration. This is good news!

POTTY PAUSE PREVENTION - GIVING THE TOOLS TO "DO IT MYSELF"

Okay, so this train of thought leads me to a key point relating to EC: potty pause prevention. In my Potty Pause section I outline many ways to stifle the pause, including understanding that sometimes it's just part of the process. And it can be! *Because they want to do it themselves.*

So, teaching some building blocks and preparing them for independence *when developmentally appropriate* can help prevent aforementioned potty pauses. Yay! This is great.

THE BUILDING BLOCKS: WHAT CAN BE TAUGHT, AND WHEN

And finally we've made it past all the philosophy and to the point of WHAT can be taught and WHEN. Woohoo! I call these the Building Blocks of Potty Independence because they set a strong foundation for the future we are creating.

Remember to teach the following skills only when developmentally appropriate (although I suggest some times that work for some folks)...and feel free to add in your own ideas that come to mind as potentially helpful tools, skills, and processes.

MOVING TO THE POTTY/BATHROOM

This may seem silly, but some kids need to learn the general direction to walk or run so they can get near the potty to eventually do their business.

You can first model the motion to the potty by airlifting your baby mid-pee during naked time while saying "wait" and then gently putting him on the potty, saying the thing you want him to eventually say to you (like "potty Mama/Papa").

I wouldn't necessarily do this prior to 9 months old, but you can choose when it feels right to begin modeling and teaching during naked time. (The reason for 9 months is that this the average age when babies begin to retain short-term memories.)

Also, you won't want to do this long, as I speak about in the Responsible Diaper-free Time section, so if you wanted to do a 1-2 day intensive modeling this action, at months 9, 12, and 15, it might help. You choose!

You can also teach your baby how to get herself *to the bathroom* when she becomes more mobile. Most often this happens upon walking.

We taught a song called "run, run, run to the bathroom" where we shuffled together to the bathroom from the other room, then added the sitting dance, up next....

TEACHING TO MOUNT THE POTTY

Obviously you can begin to teach this activity when your child is able to stand and, preferably, walk.

My dear elder friend, who potty trained her children at 15 + 18 months back in the day, suggested I teach Kaiva how to sit on the potty (we were so blocked at 13 months). It had never dawned on me! She did it with hers by sitting on it herself, to model it for them.

Since I love to dance, and my son showed an interest in that, too, we made up a dance called "back, back, squat." I showed him how to shuffle backward and squat on the pot. I also showed him how to mount from the side. We did this during a 2 day naked time experiment, and he eventually got the hang of it but only did it once himself that day. Within a few weeks, he began doing it himself more often.

We integrated "run, run, run to the bathroom" with "back, back, squat" and our son finally had the missing pieces that allowed him to claim more of the process for himself. For a toddler, this is golden.

You can also teach them how to mount the potty (or seat reducer, with stool), by having other slightly older, potty trained kids demonstrate on your child's potty. If all else fails, show some YouTube videos of other kids using their potties and "how to sit" might just click.

Remember, they are born wanting to crawl or toddle off to do their business, not knowing how to sit on a foreign object like a potty. It's a good thing to teach!

Oh, and if your child can stand or "creep" along furniture, <u>is not yet walking</u>, but shows a willingness to learn, you can have her stand in front of the potty (with her back to it) and then push the mini potty up to her calves, then say, "Ok, you can sit now."

PROMPTING AND SIGNAL PHRASES

You can also teach your child what you want them to eventually say (or sign) to you. *This will ultimately replace the Cueing noises you've been using.*

As you and your child make your way to the bathroom/potty, say the phrase. It can be simple like "potty" or "need to pee." Or it can be a sign language communication.

During the pee, not before nor after, say or sign it again to strengthen association. This can happen whenever you feel it's right…any age is okay to model the thing you want her to eventually say/sign.

PULLING DOWN PANTS (PUSHING DOWN PANTS)

One method to do this is to have your child sit on a low stool and then you pull his pants halfway down. Then tell him to grab the pants and pull them the rest of the way off.

Another way is to, instead of saying "take your pants off" or "pull your pants off," encourage your child to <u>grab</u> at the material and hold on. Then help her pull in the right direction (down).

You can also try to get a more dexterous child to <u>hook his thumbs</u> in his waistband and move them down his legs himself.

This can happen when your child can walk and has improved hand-eye coordination (This may be earlier than you think! You can experiment at different times to see.).

TEACHING A BATHROOM ROUTINE

Another thing that works for some kids is a bathroom routine. This can be fun, and young toddlers love predictability, patterns, and rhythms in their day.

An example could be: we run to the bathroom, close the door behind us, sit on the potty, pee/poo, climb up the stool (or are held up to the sink), turn on the water, lather up with soap, and rinse our hands.

This can take the focus off of the potty act and can instead be a fun way to learn a whole routine. Remember, toddlers love mastery! And doing grown-up things.

PEEING WITH PEERS...ER, TOYS

If your child doesn't have siblings or neighbors with young kids, she might want some company while peeing. It makes her feel more social, as if she can help her stuffed animals and toys pee, too.

Bring a toy along, ask him if the tractor or doll needs to pee too, or maybe if they want to pee with him, and then let them each do their thing in the potty.

This is included in the teaching section because it encourages the social aspect of pottying: everyone does it, including our toys! It can fill the community void.

NOTE: My board book for children ages 6 months and up teaches both the routine and the peeing with toys concepts through modelling and a fun rhyme. You can get a copy of that at godiaperfree.com/tinypotty.

WHEN FULL-ON COMPLETION IS POSSIBLE

It's all based on capability, *not readiness*. However, I recommend not going for any sort of completion until your baby is 14-18 months old <u>and</u> shows most of the following signs (they indicate that her brain can now hold a long-term, repetitive action and execute it regularly, which typically happens within this age range).

Per Jamie Glowacki, non-coercive potty training expert, the following are signs that your child is capable of being potty independent:

"I use 3 of 4 markers to gauge readiness:

The ABC song. Does your child have a grasp on the ABC song? I use this because your child doesn't understand the complexity behind learning the alphabet. No, your child knows this song because you sang it 600 times. They learned it by repetition and consistency. Human beings learn new skills by repetition and consistency. I repeat. We learn by repetition and consistency.

Can your child communicate, in any manner, that she needs food because she is hungry?

Can your child communicate, in any manner, that he needs fluids because he is thirsty?

Can your child throw a tantrum, for anything?

You may laugh at this, but listen: a tantrum, any tantrum, is due to your child wanting something and you not giving it. *It means your child is aware of his desires.* If your child is capable of being aware of and acting on his bodily functions of hunger, thirst and desires, then your child is capable of being aware of and acting on his bodily functions of pee and poop. Your child is ready to be potty trained."

I agree with Jamie. Once these markers are there, then completion is possible. The *capability* is there. The rest is up to you to guide.

How to Complete the EC Process

How to finish this up then? Again, just a reminder to not do this prematurely...see the last highlighted section.

Okay, so, basically, it's as simple as a major shift in *your* thinking and direction. You'll want to turn the boat around, firmly yet gently, and hold your ground.

Switch to clothing and undies instead of diapers or trainers. Trust in the process. Do it confidently and don't look back.

Continue what you've been doing already...respond, prompt, and teach him the above skills until he is able to put the building blocks into place so he can take himself. Repetition, my dear. Consistency.

It's like learning to tie his shoes, eat with a fork, walk, or put his toys up. It takes daily practice and some time set aside to focus (not hyper-focus) on it.

Start with daytime completion, and night will follow thereafter (you may still use a nighttime back-up, long as you wish).

You may have the occasional miss during this process, but keep with it, keep communicating, stay gentle yet firm, and know that even conventionally toilet trained children have accidents during changes, developmental milestones, illness, and teething.

You'll need to continue to prompt based on when you see her "peepee dance," when you know it's time, when it's convenient for the flow of your day (like when you're about to go in the car for a while, you'd prompt beforehand), and when the timing seems right (based on natural or generic timing). Honor the "no" and still stay present to other obvious signs.

Don't overdo it, but if your child is busily playing or surrounded by new playmates, you'll have to remind him at the appropriate times. They sometimes forget! Support by reminding, not questioning, but *taking* (with the tractor or doll in tow, if necessary!).

253

And REMEMBER: DO NOT OVERTALK. Overtalking smells like fear. More importantly, it leaves no room for the child to think or speak. They're not able to integrate what you've been saying if you never take a break from talking. So KEEP IT SIMPLE MA AND PA!

Just continue to do the same pottying routine, by the same predictable rhythm, day in and day out, with few words, supporting where needed, prompting when needed, and with this *consistency* and *commitment*, it will be done!

IF you need more help than these instructions here, and your child is over 18 months at this point, see the Mobile Baby and Young Toddler Modifications and Maintenance section for completion tips.

If this still isn't enough, no worries! Get my other book on non-coercive potty training (at godiaperfree.com/potty-training-book). It's got a special section dedicated to completing potty independence if you've ECed for any amount of time.

Some final words on potty independence….

POTTY INDEPENDENCE: IT'S ABOUT BABY'S CAPABILITY *AND* PARENT'S DIRECTION

By "direction" I mean "navigation." You are the parent, you are in charge, and you guide this little ship til she can guide herself. Yes, she is born knowing she needs to pee and preferring to pee elsewhere than in her pants. Beyond that, you are helping her, guiding her, as to where said pee goes, and how to sit on that contraption it's supposed to go into.

So, in summary, to move to potty independence:

1. your child needs to be developmentally/physically capable of those things you are teaching (see the highlighted section of the readiness gauges) **and**
2. you, the parent, need to be clear about, self-assured around, and committed to your direction (are you done?).

Take an honest look at whether you are unconsciously keeping your "baby" a baby...or are you honoring your emerging toddler's independence and desire to learn how to do things himself?

I guess I'm getting to this point: we are building a bridge between the pure form of EC we all started with and the inevitable approach of potty independence...be assured, firm, yet gentle about where you're going, and how.

Your baby is counting on you to be the expert about where pee and poo go. She's counting on you to eventually pass the baton. *When* she reaches that stage, she'll be longing for mastery. You can gift that to her (via these instructions)...or let her find it for herself. Either way is perfect!!

CHAPTER 3: PHILOSOPHY

EC PHILOSOPHY: USEFUL BACKGROUND INFORMATION

In this section we'll get into some background stuff that, normally, paperback books put in the front of the stack. Andrea believes in teaching this stuff last.

If anything, the information below will help you create and imagine a frame of reference for all the practical how-to's you've learned thus far.

Topics range from Definitions to Philosophy, Vocab to Starting Ages and Reasons. Read on....

DEFINING EC

Simply put, Elimination Communication is the original human infant pottying method. It is the natural alternative to full-time diapering and conventional potty training. It is a gentle, non-coercive way to respond to a baby's elimination needs, from birth, which enables her to follow her instincts to not soil herself, her caretaker, or her sleep space.

Yes, I said it.

Babies have an instinct to not pee or poo on themselves, you, or their bed. They are born disliking feeling soiled and prefer to maintain good overall hygiene.

(The instincts for poop are sometimes stronger than pee, however. Some babies don't mind occasional moisture, others abhor it.)

BABY INSTINCTS

Believe it or not, there was life before diaper dependence (even cloth dipes), and babies & parents coped just fine. For 200,000 years, human babies have always communicated their needs so mama and papa could help keep them, the bed, and the baby tidy.

Just as we crate-train puppies because they are less likely to go in their "dens" and will hold their potty needs, so also we find that babies inherently do not wish to soil themselves and actually have control over when they release. (Ever changed a newborn just to have him pee right when that diaper has been removed?)

That said, over that 200,000 years of Homo sapiens existence, various forms of "back-up" <u>have</u> been used in the place of diaper dependence, where the weather dictated it. Absorbent mosses, animal furs, soft leathers, and cotton-y plant matter have often been utilized within the swaddling wrap during the first 6 months of life in regions where babies had to wear warmer clothing. When the baby became old enough to crawl to the urinating pit or outdoor area (or when baby was held in-arms), these "back-up" materials were no longer used. Hence, they had zero diaper dependence. The back-up materials were used as a tool instead (as with EC, I encourage diapers to be used as a tool).

Cloth diapers were made commercially available about 200 years ago. This created the possibility of somewhat limited diaper dependence (limited only by the mother's desire to wash said diapers!) and babies were usually potty independent between 9 and 18 months.

Disposable diapers, invented in the late 1950's, have encouraged this average age up to the current statistic of 36 months!

Disposables have gotten really good at wicking moisture away from little bottoms...however, this simply delays the inevitable. These types of diapers (and some modern cloth versions, even) are, in fact, a bandaid.

Today's disposables make conventional potty training really difficult down the road. Although super-diapers temporarily satisfy baby's desire to have dry pants, it also teaches him that, contrary to his instincts, the diaper is the place to potty.

Babies are not wired to pee in a diaper and sit in their refuse...we teach them that. Babies are actually born ready to potty in appropriate places. The next step is a choice: show him you go a diaper or show him you go in a potty.

This is where EC comes into the picture. **EC is simply about maintaining a newborn baby's in-born awareness of, and communication about, elimination.**

BUT HOW COULD ONE POSSIBLY KNOW A BABY NEEDS TO PEE?

Just as babies "ask" to be fed, for help going to sleep, or to be held...they also ask for assistance relieving themselves away from their body, bed, and you. Babies' cries communicate many things.

Learning to respond to elimination needs is as simple as learning to respond to your baby's need for food, sleep, warmth, play, and holding.

Parents in the Western world aren't attuned to pottying needs or signals. These cries are misunderstood, at times mistaken for "colic" or unexplained fussiness that has the potential to make parents feel helpless and crazy.

In other countries, these communications have always been understood and honored…and if you look far enough back in American history, they used to be honored here, too.

Somewhere along the way, this connection has become lost to the Western world. We've become deaf to a call for a baby's basic need to be met.

We've simply lost our potty wisdom!

I certainly never considered the possibility of a diaper-free baby for most of my life. I wasn't raised that way, and neither were you.

Somewhere along the line we replaced EC with supposed convenience…"Diaper 'em up, do less laundry, put off potty training as long as you can, live the easy life."

However, this "convenience" has negatively affected our babies' trust in their instincts & ability to communicate, their overall level of hygiene, and the cleanliness of our environment. Not to mention our pocketbooks.

ALL OVER THE WORLD...EXCEPT HERE

Our fellow humans in parts of India, Africa, South America, China, and all other regions inhabited by indigenous or third world people still potty babies from day one. They never had (and many never will have) a dependence upon diapers. A few Westerners noticed this, studied it, and began adapting the practice for modern-day use...relearning an old art.

In recent years, EC has re-emerged from the archives of the not-so-distant past. And hopefully just in time!

US COMPARED TO 1/2 OF THE WORLD

Wise Westerners would agree that potty training has gotten a little out of hand on many levels including controversial training methods, length of time to completion, the fact that many children are still wearing diapers to pre-school, etc.

THE SHOCKING STATISTICS

- As of 2009, webMD.com reported the average age for potty training completion in the US is now 3 yrs old.
- Per Pediatrics Magazine, more than 50% of the world's children are potty trained by 1 year old.
- Before the advent of disposable diapers in 1959, babies in the US were potty trained by 9-18 months.

Wow. Wow. I just don't know what to say.

MANY NAMES

The Many Names for EC
- Elimination Communication (EC)
- Infant Potty Training (IPT)

- Infant Pottying
- Diaper-free
- Natural Infant Hygiene (NIH)
- Potty Whispering
- Assisted Infant Toilet Training (AITT)
- Trickle Treat (TT)

There sure are a lot of names floating around. For the sake of simplicity in our conversation, I'll just refer to the practice as EC.

By the way...I do use the phrase "infant potty training" somewhat often. I do this so that people in mainstream society will instantly know what I'm talking about. Elimination Communication isn't exactly a mainstream phrase (yet). However, I don't want to give the impression that this is a boot camp!

In my understanding of EC, there is a small amount of training necessary, but I like to consider it as "on the job training." Babies are born wanting to potty hygienically, but they aren't born knowing exactly know how to sit on a potty, remove their pants, or signal with the words we'd prefer them to use.

A handful of potty-related things do need to be taught along the way, so the phrase "infant potty training" isn't as repulsive to me as it is for some EC folks. So, call it what you like...it's your choice.

SOME SIMPLE DEFINITIONS

DiaperFreeBaby, a wonderful nonprofit dedicated to sharing about EC (and organizing worldwide EC support groups), has a lovely definition of Elimination Communication on their homepage that I'd like to share here.

> "Elimination Communication (EC) is NOT potty training. It is a gentle, natural, non-coercive process by which a baby, preferably beginning in early infancy, learns with the loving assistance of parents and caregivers to communicate about and address his or her elimination needs. This practice makes conventional potty training unnecessary."

Furthermore, their brochures define EC in this way:

> "Babies are aware of their elimination needs from birth and communicate those needs through various vocal and bodily signals. From the first few months of life, babies have the ability to consciously release their bladders and bowels when offered appropriate pottying opportunities. When we practice elimination communication (EC), we recognize their signals and enable our babies to maintain a connection with their bodily sensations."

Very nicely said!

WELL, WHAT ABOUT CONVENTIONAL TOILET TRAINING?

Conventional toilet training experts recommend waiting to potty train until your child "shows signs of readiness." Nurses are taught in nursing school that children lack sphincter control until 18 months of age, and potty training shouldn't start til then. Other "experts" claim that the child needs to initiate the process or otherwise "tell" you that he's ready to be done.

Really the truth is that sphincter control can naturally happen within the first few weeks (like my son could at 2 weeks old) and that the child must be capable of toilet training, which is different from ready (and all babies are born capable).

Also, only about 5% of kids self-initiate and complete potty training when "ready," usually between 2 and 3 years old, sometimes at age 4 when uber-socialization kicks in and they realize they're the only ones in their peer group pooping their pants.

This is all my way of saying that most of our present potty training "knowledge" is very, very questionable. In any case, that leaves many of us toilet training toddlers.

(NOTE: If you are also training a toddler age 18+ months and aren't complete yet, get my other book on non-coercive potty training at godiaperfree.com/potty-training-book and get that sorted within 7 days, non-coercively. EC is not congruent with the needs of toddlers, so a non-coercive potty training alternative is preferable at this older age, in honor of the child and where he's at developmentally.)

Anyway, we all know what stage toddlers are in: ultra-explorative, lacking attention span, and frequently using the word "No!" And how totally confusing might it be for a toddler to all of a sudden be encouraged to use a potty instead of his diaper as the toilet? Utterly. Happily…there is a way to avoid all of this calamity if you plan ahead a little bit.

As compared to conventional toilet training, EC is less coercive, less messy, less confusing, and can take substantially less time if followed with consistency, commitment, and above all else, gentleness.

Thanks to rediscovering our ancestors' (and round-the-world neighbors') ways, we can help our babies sooner than when the toddler says "I'm ready."

What EC is NOT

EC is not coercive. It is not punitive. There should be no shaming, pressure, competition, showing off, or rushing the process. EC is completely in line with babies' natural interests, needs, capabilities, preferred hygiene, and general well-being.

EC is not "training" your baby. EC is about *helping* her meet her instinctual needs for cleanliness and dryness.

EC is not "parent training." Babies only cry to communicate a need they are having in the moment...it's their only way to communicate! EC is another form of responsive parenting.

EC is not hovering over your baby all day long, waiting for him to urinate. It is, however, about helping him go when the time comes.

EC is not a chore...it's a lifestyle. It's not a fad...it's a totally different perspective, established in countless communities across the world for 100's of thousands of years.

EC is not fixing something that's broken...it's about not disturbing the natural process in the first place so that no fixing (conventional potty training) is necessary later.

PHILOSOPHY

EC is rooted in an instinctual flow of communication and an ancient philosophy.

WHY EC WORKS

EC works because it's a process based on evolutionary instinct and a natural flow of communication. EC works because parents are following the cues arising from the baby's natural flow of instincts and urgent needs. It works because it's a natural phenomenon rooted in 200,000+ years of instinctual expression.

It works because babies are born being open to absorbing our social conditioning, whether that's "pee in this diaper" or "pee in the sink" (the latter of which happens to more align with their instincts to not soil themselves, us, or their bed).

EC works because of the parents' choice to make EC a household practice (whether it's once a day or all day long). The parents' commitment is key…regardless of whether they do it part-time, full-time, or occasionally.

SOCIAL CONDITIONING

Many new parents find it disheartening when they are unable to decode 1/3 to 1/2 of their newborn baby's cries and fussiness. Most do not know that the majority of these unexplainable pleas for help are rooted in the need to pee…not that they have a wet diaper and need it changed…but that they *feel the need to pee* and need assistance to do it somewhere sanitary.

A common sentiment from parents who learn about EC later on is, *"Ohhh, I wish I'd known…."*

Alas, the baby will forgo his instincts if the parent does not listen and socializes him to "hush little baby" and "pee in your diaper (and on yourself, and in your bed…in this diaper) as I soothe you…it's okay." Over time, social conditioning causes the baby to conform to her parents' wishes. This is how we've done it for the past 60-200 years of commercial diaper use (starting with cloth 200 years ago, disposables 60 years ago).

Those who are aware of EC hear the meaning within these mysterious cries for help. They honor the baby's instinct for dryness and desire for good hygiene. They say "It's okay to need what you need and I will try my best to provide it for you when you need it." They don't necessarily do it all the time...many ECers do it part-time. But that they're *aware of* and *attempting to respond to* elimination needs is unique.

ECing parents are not by any means better than those who do not EC (especially given that most people don't even know it exists!)...it's just a completely <u>different</u> paradigm, point of view, and perspective from which to connect more deeply and work symbiotically with your baby.

WHY ECING IN MODERN SOCIETY MAY BE MORE DIFFICULT AND TAKE LONGER THAN IN TRIBAL COMMUNITY

Many folks wonder: *Why might it take 12-24 months to complete potty independence by ECing in the Western world when it only takes 6-12 months to complete it in tribal, indigenous communities?*

Some people are under the false assumption that if you do EC, your baby will be toilet independent when the natives' babies are. This may occasionally happen, but generally, this is not the case.

Here are a few theories (mine and others' that I've collected) on why it may be more challenging to do EC in Western countries.

First, in America, we not only teach the baby the *location* of where to go potty (in the bathroom) but we add the detail of *in which receptacle* they must go. It just so happens that giant toilets are not accessible to crawling infants, nor newly toddling ones...so we make tiny toilets and then teach babies to use bigger ones when they can. This complicates things and takes a bit longer.

Further, the problem with the receptacle we teach our children to use is that it requires a *sitting* position. In indigenous cultures, babies (and grown-ups) squat to pee or poo. There's something in our wiring, in our instincts, and even in our physiological make-up that determines the natural position for pottying is **the squat**. Our babies are not naked, outdoors, and squatting. They are requested to potty sitting down on a toilet like civilized people do.

Second, on the note of nakedness, the other block here is that our babies wear clothes whereas most in tribal societies do not. Babies generally can't remove their own pants (in time anyway) and underwear until they're about 2 years old (I've also heard of some as young as 15 months doing this with parents' help, but without help, 24 months is average). The tradition of clothing our babies definitely delays the completion of total toilet independence.

Thirdly, in Western society we generally live one family to a household, and most adults work at least part time (the majority full time). We don't have aunties, uncles, and older children picking up on signals from the baby that she needs to potty. For one caretaker to do the majority of the pottying for one (or more) baby(ies)...that is quite a lot of work and attention! With the support of an entire community, EC would be a breeze (as would all else regarding parenting!!).

Next, indigenous tribal people hold the unconscious and non-emotional expectation of a smooth toilet independence journey. There is no misplaced pressure, anxiety, confusion, or judgment around how/when/if the baby potties. They matter-of-factly take care of business and seem to instinctually know what to do, and how.

Lastly, with community that is steeped in tradition like indigenous people's are, the learning of generations of wisdom happens by *living in it*. No one needs to learn a technique or read a parenting (or EC) book or attend a class. You grow up "knowing" it all, and that knowledge is invisibly passed down as one of the norms of your culture. How much easier would EC be if we didn't have to wrap our Western brains around it? What if it was just our nature (like it was for all of our ancient ancestors)?

In summary, if babies were raised in the Western world wearing only a loin cloth and could potty outside at any time in a squatting position, EC would probably be easier and graduation would probably happen consistently by the 12th month. Add in the support of a tribal community of helpers and the wisdom of ages passed down via tradition…and Westerners would certainly join the other 50% of the world whose children are potty independent by age 1.

A TRIBAL EXAMPLE (BALINESE) FROM JEAN LIEDLOFF, AUTHOR OF THE CONTINUUM CONCEPT

"Then he gave signs of wanting to pee. He wasn't wearing diapers. The parents told him to go to the edge of the floor (there was no wall on that side) to go — and the child went by himself, relieved himself over the edge and came back. There was no sharpness. It was just, "This is where you go." It wasn't angry or punishing and it wasn't permissive. It was the third way — to give the child the information about what to do, because that is what social beings want to know."

-Jean Liedloff, author of *The Continuum Concept*, from an article at continuum-concept.org entitled *"Back to Bali,"* 1992

THE CONTINUUM CONCEPT, EC, & CHILD-CENTEREDNESS

The book *The Continuum Concept*, by Jean Liedloff, eloquently illustrates how the Yequana people, Stone Age Indians residing deep in the forests of South America, raise their children, emphasizing that what we *expect* of our little ones determines much of what they do and how they behave. If we expect them to fall, they do as we expected. If we expect them to potty outside, they do. For the Yequana, it's not an emotional battle *against* children for anything...it's a totally non-adversarial lifestyle.

Furthermore, you'll recall that Jean recommends strongly against a child-centered rearing in her book. She goes to much length to prove that child-centeredness leads to rebellion, to a baby who is constantly (& loudly) signaling the caregiver to "give the me the correct experience...show me how to be an adult!" Child-centeredness produces a super-grumpy child.

She recommends going on with your life as you did before having your baby, doing grown-up stuff while wearing your baby so he can witness and begin learning what it will take to be a grown-up and contribute to the society he was born into.

While doing all this grown-up stuff (shopping, laundry, cooking, walking, socializing, using the toilet, gardening, etc.), you remain receptive to the signals that your baby (in his little baby carrier, held close to your body) is constantly giving off. This builds your intuition, connection, and awareness, but not at the expense of irritating your child.

Jean mentioned that if you sit around and stare at your baby all day, asking him what he wants to do (instead of showing him what "we" do), he will become agitated and start signaling for correction. He is not signaling for more playtime with you, or because he's a "terrible two" or toddler, or because he's a willful, deviant troublemaker...it's because he wants you to show him something interesting by doing something interesting.

Within this type of setting, babies are softer, calmer, and happier. When parents EC their babies in countries where the continuum (nature's plan) is honored, they do so matter-of-factly: "This is where we pee. I believe you need to go, so if you do, go here."

The book also mentions that babies crave *information*. So, we can apply this to EC by providing our children with information about where we expect them to potty. We don't plead, we don't persuade or coerce, we don't force…these are all what Jean calls *adversarial* styles of parenting. We align ourselves with the <u>fact</u> that our babies wish to keep themselves, us, and their dens dry, and we assist them in going when they tell us they need to go (or when it's "time," or when we have an intuition around it).

Jean recommends not being permissive, so when baby pees on the floor we express our dismay but do not direct it at the child. We matter-of-factly tell them that this is not the place to go…that over there is. We clean it up without anger towards them. We continue to love the child, but we do not pretend to love the displeasing act. We teach them about right and wrong by reacting to things that displease us in an authentic manner.

Jean believed our babies are innately social and that we should expect them to do the right thing, to want to participate and cooperate with us. We don't have to convince them…we just believe. They are born social, and the book states that we mold them into becoming antisocial by our expectations that they will be bad, terrible twos, and other examples of "trouble."

By giving babies information about living (and pottying) instead of trying to force, please, or question them about what they want to do today…we give them opportunity to happily contribute to the society they were born into. We pee in the potty. That's just what we do.

A SUMMARY OF HOW THIS PHILOSOPHY APPLIES TO EC:

- Don't hover over your baby all day long waiting for her to signal….

- Go forth with your life, showing her what it is to be a grown-up from her "right" seat in the carrier, close to your heart....
- Be diffusely aware of her pottying signals and needs without hyper-focusing on her as the center of attention....
- Teach her about life, and pottying, by modeling it in your day-to-day activities and giving her matter-of-fact information....
- Do not coerce, plead, or punish; instead, help her do what humans are expected to do: pee/poo in the appropriate place....
- Let the mobile baby go along with his whims and explore, keeping an ear out for the signal, intuition, or time to go without imposing upon his deep exploration of his surroundings....
- Have an "open-door" policy in your family bathroom so your baby can get hands-on, eyes-on experience of what is expected of her in the grown-up landscape.

DISCOVER MORE...

If you're interested in reading more about The Continuum Concept, visit them at continuum-concept.org or get a copy of the book at godiaperfree.com/continuumconcept.

VOCABULARY

As with many unique things, EC has its own native vocabulary.

15 EC TERMS DEFINED

MISS

In conventional Western potty training, if a baby doesn't go in the potty, it's called an "accident."

In EC vocabulary, this changes to a "miss." Basically, you both have missed the opportunity to potty. It's not a mistake…nothing bad has happened (as "accident" infers). You just missed the communication coming to you, or missed the timing or signal, or didn't respond quickly enough. Your baby missed the opportunity to ask to go.

Examples:
"We've had several misses this morning because he is peeing every 10 minutes!"

"While I write this book, I ironically have more misses than when I'm not writing about EC."

What to do? Ask yourself what you've learned from this particular experience, forgive yourself (if you're hard on yourself), and move on with a smile.

CATCH

Another EC term is "catch." If you "catch" a pee or poo that means that you've successfully helped your baby go to the bathroom. You've "caught" the pee or poo.

Example:
"We caught a big poo first thing this morning!"

This doesn't imply that EC is about catching…it's just a term that folks have adopted to explain the opposite of a miss.

MIS-GUESS

A mis-guess happens when you believe your baby has to pee, take her to the potty, position and cue, and she tells you that she didn't have to go this time.

Example:
"I thought she had to go but I must have mis-guessed again."

Mis-guesses are valuable in that they hone your awareness of baby's actual signals and timing...and they can clue you in to when her patterns are changing.

As with a miss, ask yourself what you've learned from the situation, shake it off, and move forward with some new information!

And remember that you didn't do anything "wrong" by offering potty to a baby who didn't need to go...you are doing your very best.

PRE-PEE

Sometimes your baby lets a little pee out when she's trying to hold it while you get her to the potty place. This is called a pre-pee.

If you find her diaper or undies to be wet while you're en route to the potty place, she may still have to go. Offer her the potty despite the wetness, as this may have just been a pre-pee.

PEENIE-WEENIE

Some people call the erection that a boy gets when he's about to pee a "peenie-weenie."

Whatever you call it, it's true that most boys get a little hard-on right before peeing. Observe a newborn boy and see that it's a fact (but prepare yourself for a spray!). PS – Some boys also tug on their peenie-weenie prior to peeing.

POTTYTUNITY

Throughout your day you will offer your baby many "opportunities to potty," otherwise known as "pottytunities."

Pottytunities can be given based on baby's Signals, Generic [Common] Timing, your baby's Natural Timing, and/or Your Intuition.

They can include: upon waking, before a bath, 10 minutes after breastfeeding and then 20 minutes after that, when your baby squirms in bed, when your baby suddenly becomes fussy, when you have a thought that he may need to pee, etc.

SIGNAL

A signal is your baby's movement, body language, or certain noise that indicates she needs to go potty.

CUE

A cue is the noise you choose to make that tells your baby he can release his bladder and/or bowels. You establish your particular cue during the early days of observation, when you cue along with every pee or poo as it happens.

GENERIC TIMING

Generic Timing refers to common times that most babies need to pee or poo. Examples include at a diaper change, upon waking, and when taken out of the carseat. Also called "Transition Times."

NATURAL TIMING

In addition to the more generic times that most babies need to go, your baby's pottying also follows a baby-specific, more personal pattern. Examples of natural timing are that your baby needs to poo every morning at 6am, or that she pees 10 minutes after every feeding.

INTUITION

Intuition can take the form of a thought, emotion, physical sensation, hunch, or mental picture that is telling you that your baby needs to potty. Intuition can also take the form of a counterintuitive thought that says, "he can't possibly need to go again."

POTTY PAUSE

A potty pause happens when your baby refuses to potty and/or you experience several misses for an expanded period of time, such as 3 days of misses in the midst of a fairly regular, predictable pottying routine.

See Potty Pauses for more information.

GRADUATION

Some ECers have lessened their use of this term because "communication" is the goal of EC, not "completion," but you still may hear the term. Graduation means that your baby has completed EC and is now potty independent.

The exact definition for graduation can range from "always tells me she needs to pee and rarely has a miss" to "can take himself to the potty, pull down his pants, and wipe himself when he's finished."

You can guess that "graduation" can be a misleading, convoluted concept.

I'll leave out all the phases and stages of gradhood that I used to toss around. Although the terms may help you gather an identity within this process, they sometimes make you feel defeated, like you're never going to be done, instead of appreciating exactly where you are.

My take is this: even with conventional toilet training, accidents happen after the child is pretty much "done." These usually occur during growth spurts, teething, illness, or major family or developmental transitions. These accidents are a form of communication about the overall wellness of a child, believe it or not.

278

You will know when you're "graduated"...you won't have thought about pottying for 4 hours straight and then your child will ask to go, or you'll prompt him when you see his peepee dance. **That's when you know you're done.** You'll still be needed for the occasional prompt, and to wipe, and maybe to assist with pants, but otherwise it'll be pretty clear when this all "clicks" and the hard work is mostly done!

If you, like many ECing parents, need help wrapping up the EC process at 14-18 months, please see The Building Blocks of Potty Independence for guidance.

LATE STARTER (5-12 MONTHS)

"Late Starter" is what it's called when you begin EC with a baby who is 5-12 months old. It is referred to as "late" because the process begins *after* the first, most opportune window of starting EC (0-4 months) has closed.

I don't like to call it this anymore because it makes one feel like a loser! **You're not late. You're here now. Whatever.**

However, if you are starting EC at this age (which most of you are!), please see the Mobile Baby and Young Toddler Modifications and Maintenance section of this book for tips on how to begin.

EARLY START POTTY TRAINING (12+ MONTHS)

The late starters' EC groups say that beginning potty learning *after* the age of 12 months should no longer be called "EC" because the child is so developmentally different from a 5-12 month old. The process of potty learning after 12 months is equally different.

Therefore, at 12+ months it's not called "Late Starter EC" anymore...it's called "Early Start Potty Training" because you're starting conventional potty training *early*.

Hope this doesn't confuse you. Feel free to call it whatever you like. I do.

But, basically, the time range I'm defining here includes: *after* your baby is 12 months old but before the usual starting time of conventional potty training, which, as it's based on the child's individual "readiness," varies greatly. Therefore I've left the age range for Early Start Potty Training open-ended...as 12+ months.

Oh kay. In any case, the philosophy, principles, and processes of EC shared in this book are applicable to children beyond 12 months old (up to 18 months)...you just may need to modify some obvious details. Just know that non-coercive, gentle listening and responding can be practiced with every child.

For more information, see the steps listed in the Mobile Baby and Young Toddler Modifications and Maintenance section of this book as they also apply to those engaged in Early Start Potty Training.

WHEN TO BEGIN EC

The first, advantageous window for beginning EC is early. In fact, it's best to start preparing for EC when you're pregnant. However, there is no definite cut-off to beginning and you can start (with some modifications) at any age.

If you are able to start within the first 4 months of your child's life, it will be easier for you to integrate EC into your relationship. You will enter your rhythm together more naturally during this fresh time of hormone-enticed deep connection, resonance, and intuition. Your baby will not have been conditioned to go in a diaper and ignore her instincts for dryness. You will achieve faster and better results.

As compared to other potty training methods, this one *must* begin early...there is no waiting for signs of 'readiness' or the ability to self-train. Babies are born ready, and EC takes advantage of that.

However, people start at various times for different reasons. Wherever you are, here you start! In this book revision I've chosen to stop calling it "Late Start" and just call it "starting EC older"...but here's a chart of what others in the EC circle call things:

Age Range	What *Some* Call It
0-4 months	EC
5-12 months	Late Start EC
12+ months	Early Start Potty Training

When your baby is born, you may feel overwhelmed at the newness of so many little things...and the incredible amount of energy required...so if you're not committed, EC will fall through the cracks. Avoid this by entering into birth prepared to respond to your baby's needs and cries in this additional way.

NOTE: If you're beyond that first window, do not sweat it! 0-4 months is the "first optimum" age range, but you can begin at any age. You'll just do it differently.

WHAT "STARTING EARLY" CAN INVOLVE

Your baby asks for food on day one. Your baby asks for warmth on day one. Your baby asks for comfort on day one. Your baby asks for sleep on day one.

She also asks for assistance keeping the bed, herself, and you dry, and maintaining good hygiene, on day one.

Starting at this time is similar to starting breastfeeding at this time. Although it may be a bumpy road, it's about *beginning* to listen. *Committing* to listen. To support a little being do what he can't do by himself.

> *"But I just had a baby and am recovering (painfully) myself!"*

Well, perhaps you didn't know this, but…**you do not have to physically take your child to the bathroom on day one, or even know how. And you don't have to do it 24/7.** What I am saying is that a commitment to connecting with your baby on this level is totally possible from day one…as is starting the observation and cue cycles.

This early attention lays the foundation for the ongoing commitment that EC requires of parents. Starting on day one, even in a tiny way, can help keep you from putting off EC until it's less opportune to start.

And you're sitting around staring at your beautiful new baby all day long anyway, right?

WHAT IF YOU THINK YOU CAN'T START EARLY? YOU CAN.

If you are physically unable to start bringing your baby to potty in the beginning, **you can still begin ECing in other ways during**

the first days. You can start right away with The Basics Part 1 (which are found in the section that covers your baby's current age) and learn to notice his signals and cue along with him when he goes. By the time you are well enough to take him, you will be more in tune than if you start later…and your baby will already trust you in this way.

If you have other people helping you recover, consider asking them to help EC your baby with you part of the time. Especially for those with traumatic birth experiences and/or physical handicaps, community support in ECing is so important.

Keep in mind: if you put it off because you're telling yourself that you're not well enough to potty him, you may miss the first window of opportunity. You **can** begin by observing, learning, and cueing without having to physically take him to potty.

Yes
you
can.

I believe in you!

DO I HAVE TO DO EC 24/7?

No. No way. You can do EC as often as you like, or as little as you are able. Many people do it part-time and experience wonderful success. EC is mutually flexible and can fit any family's philosophy and work-life balance. Even those who are stay-at-home parents sometimes choose to only do EC part-time. It's totally up to you.

See my special section called Part-time EC.

BUT WHAT IF MY BABY DOESN'T "ASK" ME TO GO?

If baby, for whatever reason, doesn't give signals or "ask" to potty directly, parents can anticipate that baby may need to go and can successfully EC solely based on their baby's natural timing and also certain times of the daily routine that are opportune for pottying (generic timing or "pottytunities")…and intuition!! It works!

A GENTLE COMMITMENT

As with everything as new parents, putting pressure on yourself to be "perfect" is a sure setup for feeling like a total failure. Your commitment involves listening, responding when you can, and connecting with your baby.

Think of this type of commitment as smooth, cyclical, fluid, gentle, and flexible...not goal-oriented, linear, firm, ambitious, or tenacious.

Do your best. Love yourself and your baby. Flow with change. Keep it light. And while being light...truly commit to helping her do what she can't do for herself:

Eat. Stay warm. Relax. Potty in an appropriate place.

A TRIAL PERIOD...

I recommend trying this (giving it your "all" for at least a month...whether it's part-time or full-time) and seeing if it's for you. Pause when you feel like it's not right for you. Stop when you know it's just not working out.

If you find yourself becoming angry, resentful, forceful, or just plain stressed out about ECing, you may want to seek loving support from others or direction from an experienced parent or mentor.

At the very least, take a break for a few days and focus on connecting with and having fun with your baby & your family!

Ultimately, if you're unable to find peace within the EC process, you may simply choose to do conventional potty training when the time comes, thus focusing on *creating peace now*...knowing that you've at least tried.

SET YOURSELF UP FOR SUCCESS!

Give yourself & your baby every chance for success:
- Start early if you can (during the first 0-4 months, if not on the first day in little ways).

- Stay calm and curious.
- Do only as much as you are able and/or willing to do.
- Seek support and guidance if/when things become challenging.

WHAT TO EXPECT (OUTCOMES)

In case you were wondering, starting on day one does *not* guarantee early potty independence…however, most people find that their babies "graduate" EC sooner than they would have completed conventional potty training.

Every baby has her own unique developmental rhythm and temperament. Keep in mind that we're not doing EC in a tribal community where early potty independence is the expected norm, and everyone helps out. We are doing it within the context of modern society…and usually on our own. So…outcomes….

If you're wondering when ECers generally graduate…it can range between 6 and 24 months depending on your definition (ranging from the ability to potty on cue to total potty independence), while some say you can expect reasonable independence between 10-20 months. In any case, the average completion age by conventional toilet training methods is 36-38 months, so even the later end of EC graduation (20-24 months) is considered "early!"

Note that accidents (misses) DO happen even with a potty trained child! So, that doesn't mean you're not graduated. The need to prompt your child when she's distractable will continue much into the early childhood years…it's just your job to take the slack when things are busy, and remind her.

All said, it's safe to shoot for 20 months as a loose target. It takes up to 18 months for the brain to retain all this stuff anyway!

And remember, completion is not the goal…communication is. But even with learning to read, we do expect them to, someday, be done, and so we gently give them the tools to get there, yeah?

AN ENCOURAGING NOTE FOR THOSE STARTING OLDER (5 MONTHS +)

If you've gotten this far and are super-bummed that you may have missed that first opportune window, please don't fret! If you are unable to start until month 5, 6, 8, 11, or 16…**go for it!** It will be different and unique, perhaps challenging in ways, however, some babies respond well to beginning EC at a later age. New windows of opportunity open at various stages along the way. Many of those started older even complete sooner (not that that's our goal)!

For more in-depth help starting EC with ages 5 months and up, please see my detailed Mobile Baby and Young Toddler Modifications and Maintenance section for a comprehensive how-to…and the Resources section for more sources of direct support.

WHY IS IT POSSIBLY A CHALLENGE TO START OLDER?

Well, by this time:
- baby has been intensely conditioned to potty in his diaper
- baby has lost sensitivity to his inborn instincts for him, his caregivers, and his bed to remain dry and clean

286

- baby has lost awareness of the act of eliminating (ie: this came out of my body and made me wet?)
- the natural development of control over the associated potty muscles has not been encouraged or necessary
- baby becomes used to feeling wet
- parents aren't aware of or in tune with his rhythms and (sometimes subtle) signals, as these mysterious signals have simply been piled into the category of "unexplained fussiness"
- parents may have difficulty picking up on these signals, if the baby is still signaling at all
- and, developmentally the baby is now more interested in crawling/walking/talking than pottying.

IF you can help it and have enough notice when reading this book…start before these challenges get a chance to settle in. If not, don't sweat it!

REASONS PARENTS DON'T START EARLY

Some common reasons parents don't begin EC during this prime window are that they:
- weren't aware that EC existed!
- feel too overwhelmed with a new baby to do something as foreign as EC
- don't know exactly how to start ECing
- can't find clear instruction
- don't realize that researching potty training can happen before birth, not after the toddling begins
- don't have access to proper support or guidance
- have a toddler running around (usually in diapers or potty training) too, or multiple children
- feel skeptical or doubtful that it will work for them
- tell themselves "it can wait" or "there are more important things to attend to right now"
- aren't informed that babies will lose sensitivity even after a few months
- figure "Why bother? I'm going back to work soon anyway."

- are afraid to handle their baby in this mysterious way
- are physically recovering from birth (the Mamas), coupled with the belief that they can't begin ECing unless they can carry the baby to the potty
- are confused or intimidated by the size or complexity of the EC how-to information out there (physical books and/or websites)
- don't have time to read another book
- are pressured by skeptical friends and family to not try something so "weird"
- or even feel embarrassed to be the only one they know doing EC.

All of these reasons are based on valid feelings, realities, and beliefs, yet many of them are easily treated with the right guidance. In the absence of encouragement and proper guidance, the above reasons have become blocks for many parents. Because of these blocks, some parents decide to wait until they feel "ready" to begin ECing...usually not until anywhere from 6 to 16 months. Some wish they hadn't waited, as it is easier than it looked back then!

If you are pregnant or your baby is 0-4 months old and you are telling yourself any of the above reasons, please try to give EC a start, even in a small way, and know that you're not alone!! Many have been there & we believe in you....

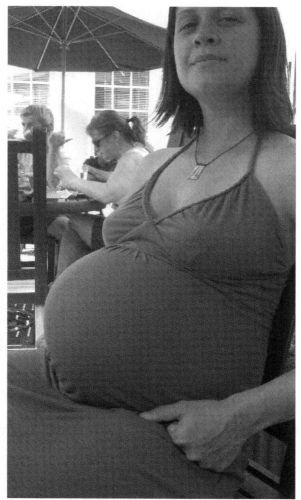

You can start learning while you're pregnant, if possible!

KEYS TO EC

These keys will help you navigate your EC journey.

13 KEYS FOR EASE & GRACE

BE GENTLE & NON-COERCIVE

EC is rooted in a natural process...mothers across millennia have pottied their babies from birth. There is no coercion necessary, no star system, points, or M&M's to be earned, no forcing or pressuring necessary to potty your baby. EC is gentle and non-coercive.

If you find yourself stressed and getting angry, please know that all parents become overwhelmed, tired, and upset at times and we all need support. Call a friend, email an EC support group, lighten up on the EC for a while. Remember what EC is all about:

Communication – Listening – Responding Gently & Promptly – Sharing the Experience of Connection!

GET SUPPORT

If you've decided to do EC in a Western country, such as the US, some would say you're facing an uphill battle. You probably don't live in a village of extended family who practically live in your kitchen. You probably don't know many people who practice EC. In fact, those who are aware that you potty your baby probably think you're crazy, seeing EC as impossible, not at all practical, and absolutely ludicrous.

In other countries, parents have the benefit of 1,000s of years of tradition preparing them for their own children's birth & care, close-knit community to help and support, and the cultural normalcy of infant pottying on their side.

Given these realities, EC in the Western world will be less challenging for you if you enlist the support of others. Please find support in the Resources section and in our Private Support Group!

LET GO OF GOALS & AGENDAS

Focusing on goals and agendas of when you desire/wish/hope/demand your child to be fully potty independent is a recipe for disaster. The pressure of agendas will result in power struggles and stress. It's okay to know that you will, and should, be done someday (it's only healthy!), and to hold that in balance, but don't let that be your prime motivator.

For example, your child will master reading someday. You don't dive into the process pressuring your child to read by next week! Remember...the "C" in EC stands for "Communication," not "Completion."

FOCUS ON CONNECTION

If you focus on Connection you will feel happier...and so will your baby.

If you hyper-focus on the EC, you will likely become disconnected from one another. If you focus on constantly renewing and refreshing your connection with each other, the pottying will naturally fall into place.

Equally, connect with yourself and take care of your own needs as a parent. A happy parent is a connected parent.

IT'S A TEAM EFFORT

The whole concept of EC stems from the baby's instincts to not soil himself, you, or his bed, and to not have to sit in filth on any of these. The key here is to continue to remind yourself...the baby needs you to help him pee. You are his partner in meeting his needs and answering his requests. If he stops asking you altogether, or starts asking in a different way, follow his lead. Respond creatively. Be a team player!

As he will always tell you (in some way) when he is hungry or sleepy, he will also always tell you when he needs, or wants, to potty (in some way). If he's too distracted to tell you, you'll pick up the slack and prompt *him*. If his communications are too subtle for you to see, hear, or sense, trust in his natural timing to guide you. Any way you slice it, EC is a team effort.

BABY WILL START TO HOLD IT, CONSOLIDATE, & WAIT

As time goes on, you will begin to notice that you don't have to be quite so quick at offering the potty.

When the newborn asks to be picked up, she can not wait for it, but after a few months she can begin to wait a little longer...likewise with pottying she will wait a little longer as time goes on.

Simultaneous to strengthening her trust in your responsiveness, resulting in patience, her muscles will also become stronger and she'll be able to wait longer and longer (especially as her bladder grows). Babies have control over their sphincters at a very early age.

Another cool thing that happens as baby gets older is that she will begin to lump her numerous pees into consolidated pees...hence transforming two smaller pees into one larger one.

CONSISTENCY BUILDS TRUST

As I've said, if you consistently (say, minimum, once a day) respond to your baby's signals to potty, he will begin to trust you. When you consistently answer cries/requests for food, getting picked up, warmth, and comfort, the trust between you strengthens. He feels less anxious, less need to cry in an extreme manner, and more ease around life in general.

If you are in the school of thought that babies should "cry it out" alone, then your baby will lose trust in you and in himself. Every cry has value. Your responsiveness to those cries, and your consistency, builds trust.

TRUST BUILDS EASE, MAKING FUTURE DISCIPLINING EASIER, TOO

When you answer baby's primary form of communication (cries), it builds trust that her needs will be met. This trust breeds an ease in

293

your relationship. The baby doesn't have to stress out wondering if you are coming or if she needs to try to figure it out for herself. Or worse yet, the baby doesn't have to shut off all communication and become complacent.

Answering baby's signals (including those for pottying) will also make future disciplining easier because baby will trust you on a very deep level. No one wants to obey someone whom he or she does not trust. Pretty simple.

LET GO OF PERSUASION & PERFECTION

Just as pushing children to eat their dinner may be linked to later eating disorders, so can pressuring EC and being super-strict about it possibly cause problems with potty training, wetting the bed, and shame/guilt/fear around pottying.

Also, EC is not about perfection or catching every single pee and poo. It's about communication and enjoying your connection…helping your baby retain his inherent sensitivity…and following his lead as his loyal teammate.

MAKE IT FUN

Lighten up, stressy-pants. This is about communication and lessening frustration and maintaining your baby's inborn sensitivity and instincts…it's not a mundane chore.

The more *fun* you have doing it *together*, the more pleasant the whole transformation to potty independence will be! Besides, life should be fun.

WHEN IT'S GROSS

Sometimes you'll get peed on. Sometimes you'll get pooped on. If you weren't ECing, I guarantee this would happen to you anyway. But since you are, take the opportunity to model that peeing and pooing are natural and normal…not gross like our society teaches us to believe. And did you know that pee is actually *sterile?*

Instead of saying "ewwww!" to your baby's natural functions, causing your baby to eventually become ashamed of herself, you can model **acceptance**. Everybody poops. Everybody pees. And, if there is pee *everywhere*, please read my section on doing naked time responsibly.

LEARNING OPPORTUNITIES

All aspects of parenting can become vehicles for learning. While ECing, you can reframe misses & mis-guesses as precious opportunities to learn about your unique baby and your teamwork together.

If you notice that you feel badly when you miss or mis-guess your baby's cue (like I do sometimes when I'm checking emails instead of paying attention), simply say aloud "Now what did Mommy/Daddy learn from this?"

And then answer yourself. For example: "Well, Mommy/Daddy learned that in the morning time, if Bubba has not pooped yet (as he does regularly), she should respond immediately to his cues and get him to the potty...instead of checking that one last email."

Say it kindly. This models for your baby that it's okay to make mistakes, and how to forgive oneself.

CHOOSING THE MIDDLE WAY

Expecting the child to use the bathroom in the proper place is fine. Forcing the child to do so borders on child abuse. Letting the child pee all over the place (permissiveness) is just as questionable.

Some parents are what I'd coin "EC Nazis" about their practice...they hyper-focus on EC to everyone's detriment. Others are completely flakey, inconsistent, and loosey-goosey about EC, which can become confusing to the baby.

Any extreme position lacks the resiliency, flexibility, creativity, & open-mindedness needed to raise balanced children. Try choosing The Middle Way.

BENEFITS OF EC

What's in it for you, your baby, and your world.

Here are the top reasons parents choose to do Elimination Communication with their babies & how it could apply to you.

OVER 25 BENEFITS OF DOING EC

USE LESS DIAPERS

Some people EC completely diaper-free from the get-go. Those who use diapers may use the same disposable or cloth diaper for hours on end, or all day. In contrast, the same people on another day may go through an absurd number of diapers because their baby won't tolerate wetness and they're having a number of misses (for whatever reason).

However…if you look at the overall impact of being completely finished with diapers at age 1 or 2 instead of age 3, 4, or even 5…you can imagine how many diapers that will save you.

SAVE MONEY

If you save diapers, you will save money. Simple enough.

Oh, and if you EC using my Quick EC Diaper method (see How to Diaper with EC), you'll need less gear and will save even more money. You're welcome.

PAVE THE WAY TO EASIER POTTY INDEPENDENCE

Ultimately, if you maintain your baby's instinct to not soil herself, you, or her bed, and as a by-product, build trust with her by showing her you'll take her to potty when she asks…your ultimate goal of a potty-independent child will be more easily & quickly within reach. When it comes time for total potty independence, your teamwork will have paid off and the final stages will be smoother.

On the other hand, if you teach her to go in her pants you will then get the honor of teaching her that, woops, she shouldn't go in her pants, but in the potty instead. That would obviously make potty training harder. More confusing. A royal struggle.

Don't get me wrong here…doing EC in modern society does not necessarily *guarantee* early potty independence. Every baby develops uniquely, at her own pace. Also, we lack the community support that indigenous tribes are blessed with, where everyone pitches in and early potty independence is just the norm. However, many babies do finish earlier with EC than if conventionally potty trained.

DEEPEN CONNECTION

Dr. Sears, pediatrician, author, and Attachment Parenting (AP) guru, teaches parents to believe in the language value of baby's cries. Each cry is a cue…a communication. When we look at it this way, we see that babies are constantly communicating. When you answer a cue, you build trust with each other and deepen your connection.

Enhancing your connection with your baby early-on will pay off like any good investment. EC is just one more way to respond, build trust, and enhance that precious parent-child connection. In this way, EC is in alignment with AP principles.

SAVE TIME

Depending on how you dress your baby (is she wearing 5 onesies or perhaps an easy-off pair of pants and long socks?), ECing actually saves time compared to traditional diaper-changing (and bottom cleaning) routines.

If you set yourself up for success by making it easy to quickly remove and replace clothing (if any), and if you are catching those obvious "I need to poo soon" signals and thus avoiding splatter-butt in the diaper (and, yes, all over the baby and his clothes)….you will save time.

LESSEN MESS

If you've ever cleaned the rear end of a baby who's just poo'd, you know just what I'm talking about. I can not guarantee that you will rid yourself of poopy diapers forever…however, most ECing families joyfully avoid the *majority* of them.

Many parents can tell when their baby is pooping…that obvious face or stare. The odds of catching poos are on your side. When you get good at catching poos, you'll save yourself the gross work of cleaning up a splattered rear.

EC lessens mess beyond the bum. It's more hygienic for baby, household, and parents, too. Many ECing parents don't own a smelly diaper pail and find it easier to clean up after baby in these ways. And boy do their babies smell GREAT!!

You might think that by doing EC you'll get peed and pood on more often…my friends who diaper their babes report that they get dirty just as often as I do.

Lastly, cleaning up *little* newborn and *tiny* baby messes is way better than cleaning up BIG toddler messes. They just make bigger, messier, smellier waste. Let's not go there….

LESSEN ENVIRONMENTAL IMPACT

Per Wikipedia, 27.4 billion diapers are buried in US landfills *every year*…making them the third largest single consumer item in the landfills. It's estimated that they take 250-500 years to decompose…but no one really knows for sure. Since they were invented in the late 1950's, that means that <u>every single disposable diaper that's ever been thrown away still lies exactly where it was buried</u>, full of waste, practically intact. Yuck.

Add in the amount of water and detergent used to wash cloth diapers every year, the petroleum to run diaper service delivery trucks, plus the chemicals, water, and petroleum used to manufacture all types of diapers and the associated diaper industry must-haves, like disposable pull-ups and intricate stuff made of plastic, and you've got a <u>big</u> environmental problem.

By reducing the number of any kind of diaper you use over the potty learning life of your child (by taking less time to complete potty independence and/or by lessening or eliminating your day-to-day use of diapers), you <u>directly</u> impact the environment. By choosing EC, you make a difference.

299

So, you might be wondering what 27.4 billion diapers look like...

Well, they weigh about 3.4 million tons...which equals about 3.4 million Volkswagen Beetle cars or **about 485,714 gigantic, 7-ton, 14,000 pound African savanna elephants...the world's largest land mammal times 1/2 million...**

1 / 2 million of these...
Each. Year. Into. Landfills.
In the United States, alone.

HELP WITH BREASTFEEDING

Did you know that breastfeeding babies typically "pop off" the breast when they need to pee or poo? It's hard to eat and potty at the same time.

Unfortunately, most women (and lactation consultants) incorrectly interpret this popping off as a sign of over-supply, overactive letdown, and low milk supply...some serious breastfeeding problems.

This misinterpretation could be contributing to countless misdiagnoses of lactation issues, when at the core of the popping off could be just a simple signal that baby wants to go potty somewhere other than your lap!

Additionally, some moms stop the feeding when baby pops off and miss the opportunity to fully nourish him. You may have better success at giving your baby a full tummy if you pause to potty, then resume the feeding.

EXPLAIN SOME "UNEXPLAINED FUSSINESS" & COLIC

When our baby was fussy as a newborn, 9 times out of 10 he was telling us he needed to potty. Boy did we learn fast. If we didn't know about our baby's natural ability to communicate about his need to potty in an appropriate place, we would never have unraveled the mysterious, and otherwise totally unexplainable, Mr. Fussypants moments.

Some babies are labeled "colicky" when really they are just being persistent and adamant about telling you they don't want to go on themselves, you, or their bed. Perhaps they are vehemently protesting the diaper itself.

Somewhere between 1/3 and 1/2 of babies' cries and fussiness actually mean "I need to go. Please help."

AVOID DIAPER RASH

With EC, the baby doesn't become accustomed to going in the diaper and sitting in moisture and feces all day...and thus diaper rash and other infections caused by unsanitary stuff on the skin are less likely.

Whether you use disposables or cloth diapers, if you practice EC along with drying any wet areas prior to replacing the diaper, you may avoid diaper rash altogether. So many do...yours truly included.

Also, diaper-free time (time spent without a diaper – in underwear, pants, or naked – which is recommended intermittently whether ECing full- or part-time) helps air out the bum and can help quickly resolve diaper rash and/or the yeast that causes it. Sometimes putting a cloth diaper back on continues the yeast growth.

Diaper-free time is a time to heal. Add in treatment with copious amounts of the magical cream I recommend in our **Gear Guide** and...problem solved.

Skip the diaper rash problem altogether by practicing EC.

AVOID CONSTIPATION

Babies have more difficulty pooing (and strain much more) while laying in a horizontal position. The most-commonly-used "Classic EC Position" actually helps your baby have a bowel movement. It also gently presses on the bladder to help the peeing happen.

Many countries across the world do not use Western-style toilets and experience much easier movements, as children and as adults, just by squatting.

The classic EC position is a "deep squat." Coincidentally, our body's elimination systems were designed to work well with that squat.

NOTE: Some solely breastfed babies poo about 10 times a day, while others only poo every 8 days…and they're both considered normal! Sometimes the babe isn't constipated, but needs every bit of juice to grow and yields no waste for a while. You'll get more in touch with all this when you practice EC.

LESSEN FRUSTRATION

The baby cries and you try to unravel exactly what he is asking for. Is he hungry? Tired? Cold? Hot? Teething? Does he need to pee?

Figuring out the meaning of just one of these various cues can save your baby (and you) a ton of pre-verbal frustration.

"Oh, that's the noise he makes when he is about to pee. Got it."

As time goes on, baby trusts that you know what he needs and you're going to help him. As a result, his cries become less intense, quieter, mellower.

Using EC is also less frustrating for the child versus conventional toilet training, which can be very confusing after years of dependence on diapers. Now that I mention it, conventional toilet training is also frustrating for the parent!

302

GET TO KNOW YOUR BABY & HIS BODY

If you know your baby intimately in as many ways as possible, your knowledge will give you incredible gifts down the line. Knowing what goes in and what comes out, when and how often, has big benefits.

By ECing, you will become more in-tune with any upcoming illnesses & developmental milestones, possible nutrition/allergy/breastmilk supply issues, and the personality development taking place in your child.

Some ECing parents have even detected Urinary Tract Infections in their babies earlier than they otherwise would have.

Doing EC gets you in touch with your baby's body so that you begin to know what is normal and what is not.

BABY GETS IN TOUCH WITH HIS OWN BODY

Babies also get the opportunity to explore their own bodies when they are diaper-free. Especially the private parts.

This helps baby develop a healthy sexual identity and perspective. It prevents the development of shame around her genitals and, ultimately, her sexuality. Many children have come to believe that their private parts are "gross" or "dirty," the source of these thoughts being years of wearing their toilet over that area.

Most ECing parents don't look or act disgusted when pottying their baby (unlike the looks on the faces of those who regularly clean poopy toddler diapers). Many are comfortable giving diaper-free time and allowing their babies to explore and experience the freedom and goodness of their own bodies.

A bit of trivia: uncircumcised boys (all boys, for that matter) have the instinct to frequently tug on their penises, which apparently helps loosen and stretch the foreskin in a natural, gentle way. Girls explore & tug too, but for different reasons.

IMPROVE COMMUNICATION

As you learn your baby's cues and respond to them, your shared communication loop improves. EC adds another opportunity to build good communication skills as the baby receives confirmation that what he expresses has value and deserves a reply, encouraging him to communicate more.

Throw baby sign language into the mix and enjoy the budding conversations!

BUILD SELF-ESTEEM

ECed babies feel good about themselves because when they cry out for help, their parents respond and try to help them. This makes babies feel valuable, that they belong in the world and are worthwhile.

ECing parents feel good about themselves because they are experiencing the joy of connecting with their babies more often than if they didn't EC (and usually, more deeply).

SEE THAT BARE BABY BOTTOM MORE OFTEN

Who doesn't want to see (and squeeze) an adorable, clean, beautiful bare baby bottom more often?! My personal favorite benefit of doing EC is that I get to see my baby's naked bum a lot of the time...and it's soft, healthy, and smells so good. I can't imagine life without seeing it all the time. But remember - do naked time responsibly by reading that section of this book!

HAVE MORE FUN

EC can be quite fun. Making faces in the mirror as she pees into the sink. Singing potty songs as you sit on each of your potties together. Going in nature, together...how exciting!

Babies follow us around, wanting to learn how to be a grown-up human. When we engage in this activity together and build connection on this level, parents and baby all have more fun.

AND YET SOME MORE BENEFITS...

- Explain mysterious sleep issues (babies often wake because they need to pee or can't settle in a wet diaper)
- Travel lighter (you won't need all those bulky diapering supplies, but you might need a portable potty!)
- Lessen future discipline challenges
- Increase mobility, motor skills, and the possibility of earlier self-dressing
- Improve the smell of baby and home
- Decrease power struggles & diaper-changing struggles
- Understand some hyperactive behavior
- Teach child to "let go" versus "hold it"

OVERALL, EC SUPPORTS...

Good health, good hygiene, breastfeeding, Attachment Parenting, Continuum Concept parenting, child's development, caregivers' development & intuition, better sibling relationships, happier babies & parents, a different perspective of babies and cultures, and positive relationships.

CHAPTER 4: TROUBLESHOOTING

POTTY PAUSES

Potty pauses, when they happen, can tremendously discourage a family whose EC journey has been relatively smooth-going. Here's more about them and what to do.

DEFINED (AGAIN)

A potty pause happens when your baby refuses to potty and you experience several misses for an expanded period of time. For example, if all is going well for 6 months and then all of a sudden you have three days straight of missing *everything*...or your baby straight-up refuses to go for days on end...you may be experiencing a potty pause.

Many differing views about potty pauses exist. Available info ranges from the possible causes to various solutions to even the belief that they don't exist at all.

POSSIBLE REASONS FOR POTTY PAUSES

Some reasons for potty pauses may be that baby is about to hit a developmental milestone (crawling, walking, talking, etc.), she is teething, she is sick, she is undergoing a growth spurt, she has a food intolerance or allergy, or she is distracted by her budding awareness of the world.

Some also believe that baby is testing her own limits, and that "potty pauses" are just part of the learning process. They are not necessarily a *failure* in EC, per se, but a sign that your baby is [healthily] becoming aware of her ability to hold it, let it go where she wishes, and decide whether or not to go at all...independence, ability, and decision-making in action! (See Article below for the whole theory.)

Some babies pause their pottying patterns because of their caregiver's energy around pottying...whether the parent is hovering or hyperfocusing on pottying, feels stressed or pressured around pottying, is anxiety or frustrated, babies pick up on it and can choose to respond by pausing. Check in with your own stress level and (hovering?) energy around pottying...you might have to dig deep to find out what you're emitting. In my opinion this reason is the top cause for potty pauses: *potty-centeredness in the parent.*

Other babies pause because of a big lifestyle shift in the family: travel, divorce, moving, job loss, parental discord, parent(s) working overtime, etc.

Lastly, a possibility that I often ponder is that Western babies will all of a sudden resist the usual potty routine because they are not raised in tribal communities where:

- there are many examples of older children pottying in appropriate places,
- infant pottying is a cultural "norm," and therefore the learning is embedded (and expected) in their culture,
- everyone helps out so the baby gets handled by a variety of people, keeping it interesting,
- babies can generally take themselves to potty outside at an early age (crawling), thus empowering them with age-appropriate autonomy so they have nothing to rebel against,
- babies are not the center of attention but are rather engaged in age-appropriate learning at all times, and are therefore more content, and
- they do not need to learn how to use or sit on a toilet; they get to squat in a comfortable position in a general area outside, not stuck trying to figure out how to independently use a strange contraption.

I wonder if any of the above contributes to babies in our culture pausing or stopping the use of the potty after many months of success? I'm eager to find out more! In any event, let's get you through one....

HOW TO GET THROUGH A POTTY PAUSE

Although it may not be pleasant to be in the middle of a Potty Pause (in conventional potty training, it's called a Potty Strike)...know that you're not alone. Here are some suggestions that experienced ECers report have helped them get through potty pauses:

1. **Focus on being a happy & peaceful parent for the moment.** Reconnect with your baby, removing your focus on EC for now. Take a nap with your baby, read books together, put her in the baby carrier and wear her around the neighborhood, sing to her. Connect!

   "When I'm connected to my baby, EC naturally falls into place. When I'm hyper-focused on EC, we're not connected at all."

2. **Back off.** You might be focusing entirely too much on pottying. See #1. Offer less pottytunities. Your baby is more than just a peeing & pooing machine.

3. **Teach a new skill.** Your baby may lack one of the pieces she needs to feel ownership over this process.

4. **Wait it out.** Remember that "this too shall pass." Usually after a few days of *whatever* (your baby's experimentation or developmental milestone) babies go back into signaling and willingly potty full-force…sometimes even better than before.

5. **Continue to prompt your baby to go.** Don't just stop ECing all of a sudden, even as you're backing off. Try to address or support the developmental milestone or teething or chaos in the home…*and* as you "zoom out" from your potty focus, continue to offer when appropriate and at the most obvious times (like after a nap). Pottying follows mood, so support your baby through the change, when needed, & it'll pass.

6. **Gently experiment with different locations, environments, receptacles, positions, and/or cue noises.** Get creative. Sometimes it's just a simple fix…your baby's pottying preferences may be what's shifting. Change it up and see what happens.

7. **Seek support.** Come to the Private Support Group (gain access at godiaperfree.com/upgrade) and tell us what's going

on. So many parents don't ask for help. Whatever you need, seek it out.

8. **Be easy on yourself.** The pressure you put on yourself or your baby during these times will just make it worse. Be gentle, inside and out.

9. **Don't take it personally.** It isn't your fault. You didn't do anything wrong. Something's simply out of balance. Never blame yourself…your baby is communicating something by pausing. Try to distance yourself from the problem and observe it from afar, non-emotionally, perhaps with the help of a friend or your partner.

10. **When you find yourself totally frustrated, notice *I'm frustrated!*, take a deep breath, and regain your center.** Remember the long-term goals you have around your connection with your baby. This is a tiny sliver of time as compared to a lifetime with her!

11. **Avoid coercion, punishment, anger directed at your baby, and general upset.** They don't help. Take care of yourself so you don't find yourself going to these extremes. When you do feel negative emotions (we all do sometimes!), breath deeply and take a moment to regain your center.

12. **Laugh often.** It's just a potty pause. Be happy that your baby even potties at all! Most of all: stop counting your miss:catch rate. Got you, didn't I? Instead: grateful smile. :o)

AN ALTERNATIVE VIEW ON POTTY PAUSES - JUST PART OF THE LEARNING PROCESS

Next you'll find an article written by Kerste Conner, long time DiaperFreeBaby Mentor in Seattle, WA. Enjoy this fascinating and mind-opening discourse on the other meanings of a potty pause.

EC Phases
by Kerste Conner, long time DiaperFreeBaby Mentor in Seattle, WA

"I've noticed that there seem to be two times in a child's life with EC when problems arise. And I think that during both of these times, it is frustrating for the adults involved (and also for the child involved, but they can't tell you clearly) and with life being busy, it is easy to decide to put the diapers back on and wait until things improve. However, it would be better to continue doing what you are doing – **this time of discord is very important to the process** and even though there may be more misses, this is a time of great strides for a child.

When your child begins to walk or talk, they stumble and stutter and make mistakes. You wouldn't see your child struggling to walk and then think – she's not ready to walk yet (cuz she isn't perfect at it yet), so I am going to confine her to a safe environment where she cannot walk and I will keep her there until she is ready to walk. Instead you do what you can to keep her safe while she stumbles and falls and learns to teeter and totter and finally eventually walk. She fails while she is learning and as parents we tolerate these failures because we know it is part of the learning process.

However, when it comes to the EC process and we've been having success, somehow as **our child begins to learn that they are a part of the process and they can control both when and where they potty,** parents become confused – why is there now failure when before there was so much success?

I think what we fail to realize is that our measure of success needs to change at this point.

Children learn how long they can hold the contents of their bladder by holding it so long, they can't hold it any longer.

They are in touch with the elimination process, they know what it feels like when their bladder is full, but what they don't know is – how long can I wait before it is too late? They get involved with other activities and they don't want to stop, even if they have that full bladder feeling. They may be involved in this experimentation process when, based on timing or intuition, an adult decides to potty the child – who protests vehemently. Then as soon as you take the child off the potty, they realize that they have exceeded their potty-holding limit and they pee on the floor. **The adult reaction is frustration – why is this happening? But in fact, the learning process is happening.** And this is a great time to continue your communication with your child – "Oh, you are peeing. Next time, if you let me know, I can help you put it in the potty." Very low key.

So my theory is that this part of the learning process happens sometime between 7 and 12 months. What we did during this time was try a few different locations (mini potty, then sink with mirror, regular toilet with insert, then outdoors). We were trying to distract her from her bladder holding experiment long enough for her to pee. If she peed, great, if not, we used either diaper back up, or we put her on some sort of impervious surface, or lived dangerously, knowing that we'd be cleaning up a miss in the near future. Sometimes she surprised us and held it much longer than we suspected that she could – and we both learned. Sometimes she peed almost as soon as we let her go back to her chosen activity – and we both learned. The process smoothed back out again for a time, but our success rate was probably never as high as it had been before our daughter learned that she could delay the inevitable, if it suited her.

Then between 12 and 16 months, the misses begin to increase again and for us this was the real key to our daughter graduating. She became very resistant to us ECing based on timing (which we had done from birth with her). Although we had been signing with her and talking with her about elimination throughout our journey, at this stage **she was really acting out that she wanted control over this part of her life.** It resulted in quite a few misses, but instead of diapering her back up and waiting until later when we thought she was ready, we gave her MORE control, instead of less. We would ask her if she had to potty (when we thought she should have to go, or if we were heading out for a trip) and if she gave us a negative response, we would believe her (even if we were skeptical) – we allowed her the ability to have confidence in knowing her body.

Even if, sometimes, it turned out that she was wrong, the amount of time that it took her to realize that this was her thing and we were no longer the ones in control of where and when she pottied...**she was completely diaper free within one month**, and about two and half months later, she is completely miss free.

I'm not saying that this time table will apply to everyone. My point is just this: When a child who is on the EC journey has a series of misses, **instead of considering it a "potty pause" maybe consider it as part of the process** and that <u>the child is really expressing that they realize they are part of this process</u> and <u>support that</u>, instead of backing off and diapering them up and waiting – sending them mixed signals that they aren't trusted to learn this skill because it is simply too messy."

Thank you, Kerste, for your awesome article and your heartfelt contribution to the world of EC!

Sometimes it's just time for the older baby to have more control...to be given more of the responsibility and the building blocks towards independence.

A final note: You can show him how to sit on the potty, how to wash his hands, help him bring himself to the potty...grant him more autonomy while teaching the basic potty tasks found in this book when he seems to be asking for more of them (through pausing!).

TROUBLESHOOTING

Sorting out the kinks.

This section may seem redundant compared to its sub-sections and even the rest of this book...but that's on purpose. You see, many of the things I list here are useful solutions for various challenges!

If your question is not answered on the next several pages, hop on over to our Private Support Group (gain access at godiaperfree.com/upgrade) to get some support, or see the *expanded* Troubleshooting Section of the Readers' Area on our website. :)

Here are answers to the top EC questions….

OUR EC HAS STOPPED WORKING

Baby stops signaling, you miss nearly every potty throughout the day, diapers are piling up, or things just aren't working anymore.

What to do?
1. Back off a bit, while staying consistent. You are probably being potty-centered (we all do it) and causing unconscious pressure. Offer less pottytunities and connect more in other ways.
2. Focus on connecting with your baby and on nurturing yourself. A happy, connected parent makes EC flow more smoothly.
3. Remember that the learning curve is NOT straight. It is mysterious and ambiguous. Gently stay the course.
4. Experiment with new positions, environments, receptacles, and cues.
5. Review The Basics and start learning each other again. (Just don't over-do naked time.)
6. Wear your baby more often and consider co-sleeping if you aren't already. Both of these practices bring you closer to your baby's needs.
7. Check in with yourself. Are you too busy? Have you begun to tune baby out? Are you still present and listening or have other things taken your attention? Are you getting enough rest? Are you stressed?

8. Sing, take deep breaths, and help baby (and yourself) relax.
9. Read the special section in this book called Potty Pauses for info on EC breaks that are many days long.
10. Check your clothing & diapering strategies and see if they support EC like you want them to or if they need tweaking...see the sections called How to Diaper with EC, Do I Have to Do Away With Diapers?, and the Supply List for more ideas.
11. Reach out to your support groups (see Resources for a list)...tell them what's going on and ask for suggestions. Go to the Private Support Group (gain access at; godiaperfree.com/upgrade) and ask us!
12. Realize that babies are constantly morphing, learning, exploring, growing, and experimenting. Trust that your baby will get back on track in her own way and on her own timetable. Gather information, relax, and don't worry.

My Younger Baby Cries Every Time I EC

Babies generally do not cry because you are helping them potty, but rather because the act of peeing or pooing is unfamiliar, uncomfortable, and/or scary for them. Keep in mind that your newborn has been in the womb for 9 months and hasn't had to feel that strange new sensation....it can be plain weird for the first few months.

Babies also sometimes cry during pottying because they are fearful of the position you have them in. They may feel unsteady, uncomfortable, cold, or unable to figure out how to release their bladder.

Solutions?
1. Find a better position that baby can relax in. Try the Cradled Classic EC Position instead of just the Classic. See the Positions Gallery in this book for position alternatives. Remember that preferences for certain positions may change as baby grows older.
2. Sing a soothing song while pottying to help chill baby out (we like "Twinkle, Twinkle").

MY OLDER BABY PROTESTS WHEN I OFFER A POTTYTUNITY

Babies protest in order to get you to change *something*. Whether position, environment, or, hey, I don't need to go right now, here are some tips for dealing with protest:

1. Oftentimes, a little change of scenery or position helps baby release her bladder:
   - try a new position
   - try letting baby sit on her own (if she can)
   - try a new environment (sometimes going outdoors helps - but don't make it a habit)
   - try a new receptacle.

2. If your baby is arching her back and straightening her legs, she may not need to go right now. Try again later. **Never force a baby to stay in any position.**

3. Developmentally, your baby may also be interested in his new unfolding world and all the things he wants to explore. In this mindset, he is distracted by shiny objects and would rather investigate those than potty. Be patient. It'll pass.

4. An older baby may also be learning that she can now determine when and where she goes. Be patient. She's experimenting.

5. Try reducing your Timing-based potty offerings and allow baby the space to look to you, on his own accord, when he needs help...instead of swooping him away from what he was engrossed in exploring when (unbeknownst to you) he was not ready to go yet. Remember that, as babies get older, they begin consolidating their pees and poos.

6. Let her go diaper-free (or in undies/training pants) for an hour or so to reconnect with the elimination process. When she goes in an undesirable place, gently airlift her to the potty while saying "wait" and when on the pot say "pee in the potty" or "I need to pee Mama/Papa." Do this responsibly.

7. Let an older baby have more control over the process. Trust his growing intuition and bodily awareness. If he protests, tell him to tell you when he needs to go so you can help him.

8. Briefly carry baby around after a protest then try again, nonchalantly.

How Do I Aim This Thing? (Boys)

Here are some tips on aiming penises (for various ages), adapted from various EC Yahoo! Group posts.

For a series of photos of positions & methods that will help you aim your boy's penis, see the Positions Gallery.

Any Age

1. In the classic EC position, you can reach up between his legs with your index finger and physically help him direct his stream into the receptacle.
2. Hold your baby in the classic EC position over a small potty between your thighs. Tip the potty towards you and lean slightly forward to aim your baby's penis downward into the potty.
3. Try to aim his body towards a larger receptacle (sink, toilet, bathtub, outdoors).
4. If you have some time to keep him diaper free for a while, his pee stream will be straighter, as opposed to having him squished up in a diaper where the stream will become more of a spray. It's also easier to tell if a boy needs to pee when he's diaper-free because you can see his "peenie-weenie" (tiny erection).Face him towards the back of the toilet when holding him over the toilet or on a seat reducer.
5. Try the in-arms standing position at the sink, bathtub, or outdoors.
6. Potty outdoors in any position.
7. Place a towel on the edge of the bathtub and hold the baby sitting on it. Cue him and the pee will end up in the bathtub and any spray will be soaked up by the towel.
8. Use a potty mat under your potty receptacle or area to absorb sprays or spills.
9. Use a small bottle or jar as a receptacle, placed over/around the penis, catching all the spray.

Sitting & Older Babies

1. Invest in a mini potty or toilet seat reducer that has a good, tall lip.
2. Drape his lap with a prefold diaper or washrag while he sits on the potty.

3. Hold your hand over him, like a cup, to direct his stream from spraying (yes, you will get peed on...it's sterile!).
4. Help your baby lean forward on the potty/seat reducer to aim his penis downward. Be sure to sit him far enough back on the potty to have room for the pee stream to go into the potty.
5. Allow him to practice aiming through the natural exploration of his penis as he urinates.
6. Talk to your baby about the expectation of the pee going into the toilet or potty. "Point your penis in the potty. That's where the peepee goes."
7. Try holding your older baby in an "airplane" position over the toilet.
8. Let him practice aiming in the great outdoors (with Papa demonstrating).
9. Try floating a piece of toilet paper, tissue paper, or an O-shaped piece of cereal in the potty for your older baby to practice aiming.
10. Use food coloring to color the toilet water and have him practice aiming while changing its color.

WE'RE IN POSITION & CUEING BUT NOTHING IS HAPPENING

1. Try singing or deep breathing on baby's head. Sometimes baby is distracted or holding his sphincters and needs help relaxing or focusing.
2. Run the water if you are pottying at or near the sink.
3. Give baby a potty-time-only toy to play with while sitting on his mini potty.
4. Try a different environment, position, or receptacle. If you can, go outside and squat with her.
5. If he arches his back and straightens his legs, he clearly doesn't want to go (whether he needs to, or it's time, or not) and it's best to wait til next time.

MY BABY WON'T SIGNAL
(OR SUDDENLY STOPPED SIGNALING)

Don't give up. It doesn't mean she doesn't get it or that EC won't work for you (or that you are a failure). It just means that one of the 4 Roads to Pottying is not-so-dependable, and you, my dear parent, must utilize the other 3 Roads while providing repetition and consistency (without overdoing it). It's all good.

Until your little darling starts signaling to you consistently, you'll still need to prompt her by reminding her it's time. If you stop prompting altogether, she won't ever pick signaling back up. How to prompt?

Instead of asking if she needs to go, or expecting for her to Signal out of the blue (when you know she doesn't), you'll just take her. You will take over her (lack-of-)Signaling by Prompting her while you gently guide her back to health and self-sufficiency. Also, you'll want to teach her *her* future signal to her by prompting her *with* **what you eventually want her to say <u>to you</u>**.

So, here's what this looks like:

> You're enjoying your day, keeping an ear out for her nonverbal signals (that "peepee dance"). You're also loosely aware of her natural timing. And, you're incorporating the generic timing as a natural rhythm to the day. You know when it's time.

> Then...you prompt by just taking her whilst saying what you want her to eventually start saying to you, such as "I need to peepee Mama/Papa" or simply "potty" (or signing...whatever communication ability your child has, match that as a goal of how you want her to start telling you she needs to go). She'll eventually pick it up and realize that this is what we say when we need to go pee...and she will begin signaling eventually!

Remember that this is age- and capability- specific...newborn babies pretty much all signal (because their primary signal is crying), and yet eventually this may dissipate as baby comes into being in the world.

At older ages, some babies are able to verbally signal from 9 months with words, others are better with signing, and still others are just late bloomers on the direct communication circuit and you'll have to count on other factors to get you through the vast majority of toddlerhood.

Honor your baby's different pace, and **model** the desired end result (the Signal) with consistency and patience.

AND about the prompt: Be brief (one word is fine), don't over-explain (or explain at all), don't get stressed, and don't expect her to EVER say it.

What!?! Yes. Don't expect her to EVER say it. If she does, great. If she doesn't, whatever. Point is that she KNOWS in her tiny developing brain that this word means "it's time to go." This is her future signal. She gets that.

She will adapt it as she wishes and will begin to communicate it when her **brain** is capable of doing so (14-18 months is when the brain can do long-term repetitive memorized tasks *consistently*).

Usually, lack of signaling can cause an utter feeling of failure to arise, coupled by extreme potty-centeredness. These are reflexes but they won't help! What will? Patience, consistency, and repetitive prompting without overdoing it or becoming potty-centered. It's all a balance.

I AM SO FRUSTRATED! HOW DO I DEAL WITH MY OWN FRUSTRATION?

Speaking of frustration...boy have I got stories.

Know that frustration happens. To everyone. As parents, we all feel it from time to time. There might be times that you *want* to coerce your baby. And you may get very upset when he pees on you or your couch or the bed.

It's totally natural to feel that way, especially when you're wanting cleanliness, ease, and harmony in your home and with your baby. The key is to *notice your frustration* and "come back to center," again and again.

We are never going to be perfect, but we can always heighten our awareness and come back to our highest self...our center....when we notice that we've become frustrated.

How to relieve your frustration? Leave your baby with someone (or in a safe space) for a few moments and take a few deep breaths. Check in with what you're needing or wanting right now; with how you're feeling. Give yourself some love and compassion.

Of course you feel that way right now. Yes, you deserve what you're needing.

Remind yourself that parenting is often challenging (especially when doing it alone). Find some community to help support you through your frustration. Find a way to do something *for yourself* every day.

Remember: EC isn't about perfection. It's about being with what is, responding to it, and doing your best with what you've got.

My Baby Refuses to Leave Playtime to Pee

Take that tractor, that doll, that Slinky, that block, with you! Instead of "let's go pee" or asking your child, say, "I think the tractor needs to go peepee. Let's go see!"

Run, run, run (even if you are the only one running, while baby rides along) to the potty. And then have your young toddler "cue" the tractor over the potty (or demonstrate this for her).

Then confidently say "ok, your turn" or "the tractor wants you to pee, too" or "show that tractor how *you* go peepee."

My Child Withholds his Poop When I Take Him, or Stops Pooping and Won't Continue

If your (usually older) babe holds her poop when transported during or right before you know she's going to poop, try one of these two things:

1. Try returning to the in-arms EC Classic Position over the big toilet to see if the position helps it come out.
2. If #1 isn't an option, bring her to the potty and put a short stack of books under her feet...enough to straighten the colon a bit and create a deeper squat, since a deeper squat always helps! And be prepared to read, too. It couldn't have gotten too far back up that canal. It's gonna come out, just wait a sec and read and relax her.

(IF you have time between seeing the signal and him actually going) When you see him get into position and start to get quiet, pick him up and walk for about a minute or so, in a relaxed and calm manner, and make your way over to the potty.

Sit him down on it and sit next to him on the floor, making the cue noise you've been practicing or saying nothing, even averting your eyes if you choose (some prefer more privacy). Breathe deeply. Get calm and relaxed yourself.

If he doesn't go for it right away, walk him around a bit more. If he insists on running around free, keep an eye on him and note a second try to poop on your floor / in his pants. Then transport him again. Eventually he'll get the message.

I'm Catching All the Poos, But Not Many of the Pees

You're not the only one!! Know that pees are so often between age 0 to 18 months that you'll probably miss a bunch...although some kiddos begin major pee consolidation at 3-4 months, and some are just easier than others.

We always went for 50% (he peed every 15 minutes for goodness' sake!). If my son peed in his diaper back-up without telling me, he'd most definitely tell me the next time *beforehand*...so we got 50% from months 0-9. Then we got less! Then we got more again. And now we get about 99% of them (22 months) by his signal and own sense of responsibility.

Here are some point-by-points:

1. For your sanity, first of all do not strive for perfection. Let that crazy idealization go right this instant. Stop counting your catch vs. miss rates! Especially with pee.

2. Keep her in some sort of clothing or back-up while the pee is happening at such a high frequency. Remember "diaper-free" doesn't mean "naked and peeing everywhere." You're still communicating, right?

3. When babies are bored, they pee more. This is moreso when they get into the crawling/toddling stages. When they are engaged, especially with other children, they hold it more. Please don't take this as advice to spend all your time playing with your child. As I've mentioned, child-centeredness can annoy a baby. Use your judgment. Other kids are usually much more interesting to them, as are walks in nature and outings.

4. As EC becomes his normal routine, and if you use a back-up, he will begin to prefer to be dryer and will hold it more. Things definitely change over time, partially due to more control over the muscles, and also depending on what's going on in his immediate environment.

5. You gotta let a few happen. You aren't teaching her to pee in her diaper. You will likely get a better pee signal if you let her pee in her diaper the first time and if she doesn't tell you about it, the next time she needs to go she *will* tell you because she doesn't want to double-wet it. And she won't want you hovering over her all day, so holding it becomes a grand idea.

   I don't mean to stop offering, or to fore-go the best pottytunities. Just lay off a bit and offer half as much. Trust her to learn, too.

6. Lastly, if you ARE taking him all day long, he WILL pee all day long. Take him LESS.

HOW DO I GET MY BABY TO STOP PEEING ON THE FLOOR?

A horrible side effect of some of the EC information out there is that lots of babies are stuck in a rut about peeing on the floor. It's become habit. And why? Well, because diaper-free became a status symbol that "naked bottomed" represented most fully.

So...that history aside, if your baby is hooked on peeing on the floor, this is how to remedy it:

1. Start by using a back-up and/or clothing during all the awake hours. Swallow any pride about having a "diaper-free baby" and remember that "diaper-free" means free from exclusive dependence upon diapers. Using a diaper as a back-up is legit if you still practice the EC. Using trainers and undies and just-pants all count too. Stop that nakey time. Except...

2. Do a full-on naked day for one to two days, max. During this naked day transport your baby to the potty every time she pees. Turn your computer, phone, Facebook...OFF. Play with your babe but don't hover. When that pee comes out, gently say "wait" or "stop" and transport, mid-pee, to the potty saying "pee goes in the potty now."

3. In the morning say "You're wearing __ (pants/trainers/etc) ____ today and I'd like them to stay dry. Tell Mommy/Daddy when you need to pee and I'll help you." Or just say, "Let's keep these dry, k?!"

4. You can do a re-set, using the diaper as a tool, if you wish. Learn more at the end of the Mobile Baby and Young Toddler Modifications and Maintenance section.

5. Bottom line, mainly just don't allow your child to pee on the floor anymore. "Pee goes in the potty now." And help her learn how to help you help her do just that.

MY BABY WILL NOT SIT ON THE POTTY ANY MORE / LONG ENOUGH TO GO

If you can't get him to sit on the pot and pee, then catch that pee in *something*. My potty trainer friend likes to use a Red Solo Cup. Try it and see if he or she can pee in it instead. Works for some!

As a first option, try this: when you take your child to the bathroom, close the door behind you, remove his pants, say "please put your pee in that potty" and point, then pretend to do something else. He might just sit without all the attention on him.

Otherwise...For poos, and even sometimes with pees, you may need to snuggle your baby while gently holding her on there.

When you get the signal or see the pee/poo dance, sit your baby down on the potty and say "poo goes in the potty." If he tries to fuss out of it or stand up, hold him there in a snuggly warm hug, saying "This is how poo goes where it belongs. Thank you for sitting." Stroke his back, get close, sing to him.

It's kinda like gently holding your flailing, screaming, rebelling child on the car seat as you strap her in while she's struggling like hell to get out. It is for her safety, and you are not hurting her. You are taking charge in a way that is caring, healthy, and necessary.

Sometimes with pee and poo, it becomes the case of dire need. It is time. You *need* to sit for your hygiene, and your mental health.

Sometimes at night, when he was a young toddler, I had to hug my baby boy (who was not-so-cuddly) to get him to stay and finish his business (pees). For poop, the instinct IS stronger to sit and squat, so *trust* that your child, once firmly encouraged, will get it and continue with consistency. If you need to show him how to squat, do so.

Just get the message across gently, firmly, and consistently, knowing in your heart that it's best for him to pee and poo in the potty, not on the floor or in his pants. He will follow your lead.

WE DITCHED THE DIAPERS BUT HE KEEPS WETTING/SOILING HIS UNDIES/PANTS!

Whether you are "starting EC older" or have been doing so from birth, when you make the plunge to ditching diapers sometimes there's a period of wetness that might have you doubting everything.

First, I recommend a day or two of "teaching." Teaching in this case means 1-2 days of pure naked time where you transport him to the potty every single time. See the Hybrid Plan download in the Book Owner's Area for the details on doing the naked teaching time.

If you are having extreme trouble with this, then you should go back to using the diaper as a back-up and offering the potty at times that seem right: after waking, during a diaper change, when you see the obvious signals, upon intuition, or based on his natural timing. Do NOT stop EC. Just use the diaper as a tool until there is more reliability (be it signals, timing, or intuition!).

Once your child becomes cooperative with this, and you guys hit a groove, and you as parent feel confident with it, then you can ditch the diapers and have more success with the undies/pants."Diaper-free" doesn't mean ditching diapers when diapers are still needed, when they are still a useful tool. EC can be done with a diaper back-up, and most often is. The vast majority of ECers do it with a diaper back-up and have success.

One of my reader's mothers is from India and reports that they only move from the diapers of early months to the tiny underwear when the child is somewhat reliable (again, with signals, timing, or intuition).

When starting EC older (with a toddler especially) I *highly* recommend doing the 1-2 day naked time of teaching.

And from then on, yes, unfortunately the pants and undies will probably be soiled and wet for a while, could even be a couple of weeks or months (remember, the brain has to catch up!), so use the "appropriate," corresponding back-up for YOUR nerves and stress level to be under control, while continuing to work the process.

When the misses in pants/undies do occur, LEARN SOMETHING from it and do NOT let your stress show. Communicate in simple short phrases. Have them help clean up instead of playing with the pee.

At 9 months when I was sick of the diapering struggle our son proceeded to have wet Gerbers for like 4 months!! He eventually got it.

And, during the months of pee showers, we increased our catches as we gave him *more* tools such as how to run over to the potty and how to sit on his own, yet most importantly we stayed **consistent**. It was better to wash countless undies than to use diapers, for us, and it wasn't easy. I had to keep my patience level in check constantly.

MY CHILD TOTALLY GETS IT ALL, BUT KEEPS PEEING ON THE FLOOR

Time to stop talking so much. Plain and simple. She knows where pee and poo goes. She knows how to ask you for help. She may even know how to get her pants down. When you over-talk, you leave no room for her thoughts and her ability to act on those thoughts. Plus, hearing it over and over again will NOT help her. What will?

Begin to use simple directives, without a lot of explanation. "Time to pee." "Pee in potty." "Put your poo in the pot." Then be quiet to give your child room to process the information for herself. (And maybe check out my info on The Building Blocks of Potty Independence.)

HOW DO I COMPLETE EC? OR "MY CHILD IS OVER 18 MONTHS AND I'M READY TO BE DONE!"

EC is wonderful. And amazing. And when it comes to toddlers over 18 months old, it becomes counterproductive if the ending steps aren't falling into place naturally. This is because they are developmentally in a different place now, and need more firm closure to the process.

If that resonated with you and you've got an over-18-month-old and want to wrap up your EC practice, but you somehow missed my instructions about how to place the Building Blocks of Potty Independence...you may want to go get my other book on non-coercive potty training (at godiaperfree.com/potty-training-book), which features an entire section dedicated to completing the process if you've done some level of EC with your child. (This doesn't exist elsewhere.)

Btw, the average completion timeline of my potty training method is currently 7 days (if 18-20+ months). And if you want personal hand-holding, get our private potty training support group. If you're ready to be done with EC, you can be. Without pressure, M&M's, or crappy gimmicks. Yay!

HOW DO I KNOW WHEN TO SAY WHEN?

Whether you choose to continue part-time or full-time, assessing your situation and choosing to re-commit prepares you for the continuing journey.

Assess Your Experience
- Are you smoothly sailing?
- Are you loving the process and deepening your connection with your baby?
- Are you overwhelmed by new motherhood but enjoying giving EC a try anyway?
- Are you stressed more often than not?
- Are you feeling lost and not getting the hang of it?
- Are you just plain angry about pottying most of the time?
- Do you need more support?
- Are the misses so many that you doubt this will ever work for you?

Going Well?
If things are going relatively well and you're enjoying the process with your baby, <u>re-commit</u> and continue forward.

A Bit Stressed or Stumped?
If you are a bit stressed or stumped and finding that you're frustrated more often than not...start over with The Basics and/or hit the re-set button.

Additionally (and this is key), seek more support. Ask questions in our Private Support Group (gain access at godiaperfree.com/upgrade). Find supportive folks to chat with. See my Resources Section for more sources of support.

Totally Stressed, Bummed, or Even Angry?
If you're just plain not getting it and/or you find yourself stressed, angry, or majorly bummed out...**get support immediately**. Tag me

329

in our Private Support Group. Additionally, it may be time to pause or possibly stop altogether.

Get Support
Find some people to talk to and express your situation, asking for support, guidance, answers, a shoulder or an ear. See Resources for support sources.

Pause
Pause for a few weeks and start again. Then re-set with The Basics...and/or a re-set. See if your emotions around EC have shifted to the positive side. If so, get some support and hang in there.

Stop
If you've tried to get support, paused and re-set, and your emotions are still overwhelming you (and your baby) with bad vibrations...by all means, throw in the towel, proudly. *You tried your very best and you should pat yourself on the back for that!*

If You Decide to Stop
If you decide to stop ECing, try to retain the basic principles around communicating gently and non-coercively with your child. This 'way of being' will support your relationship in so many ways.

If you are able, try to continue diapering in a way that maintains her sensitivity so when you're ready to move toward potty independence in a conventional manner it will be easier for you both.

WAS YOUR QUESTION NOT ANSWERED?

Hop on over to our Private Support Group (gain access at godiaperfree.com/upgrade) and get some support, or see the *expanded* Troubleshooting Section of the Book Owners' Area on our website.

330

THANK YOU!

I HOPE YOU'VE ENJOYED READING MY BOOK!

If you wish to share this book with others, please simply pass on this link: GoDiaperFree.com/thebook . By sharing this link you are helping a stay-at-home mom stay at home and I appreciate that more than anything!

Stay updated and keep reaching out for support by visiting me at GoDiaperFree.com for my blog, videos, resources (support!), and gear recommendations. If you are signed up for my email newsletter, I will send you periodic helpful Tips and Tricks and promise not to ever spam you. Or, you can sign up to have my blog posts emailed directly to your inbox.

Lastly, I want to take a moment to reflect that just by reading this book you have made steps toward enhancing the communication and connection within your growing family.

No matter what the outcome, I am happy that I get to live in this world with folks like you! Happy ECing!

SHARE, EARN, AND HOST.

Please help other new parents learn about infant potty training. It's never too late to start, 0-18 months, and most parents would have practiced some bit of EC had they known about it sooner! Please **share this link with your friends**: godiaperfree.com/thebook.

You can also help spread the word about EC *and* earn a commission for every tracked sale you refer to us! For more info visit godiaperfree.com/referral-program.

Lastly, **if you're interested in hosting a local EC group** in your community, and earning some cash in exchange for your teaching and consultation services, you may want to consider enrolling in my popular **Go Diaper Free Certified Coach Training Program**. New classes form all the time and are available worldwide. Learn more at godiaperfree.com/coachprogram - and make an impact teaching others EC, just like I do.

THANK YOU!

LEAVE A REVIEW.

If you've enjoyed this book, please hop on over to Amazon and leave a review. It is much appreciated.

I wish you only the best with your baby! Stay in touch.

xx

Andrea

PS - Again, you can feel free to reach me @GoDiaperFree on Twitter or on Facebook.com/GoDiaperFree, or email me directly at andrea@godiaperfree.com. I'd love to hear from you!

THE END

APPENDIXES

APPENDIX 1: SUPPLY LIST

Although EC-specific supplies are not necessary by any means, having some of these items can make it easier for you and your baby to practice EC.

All of the supplies I recommend are things that I've found to be useful, many of them indispensable, on my EC journey. I use or have used every single item listed in this Supply List. I searched long and hard for some of this gear to save you the hassle of digging.

Please visit *godiaperfree.com/supplylist* to download the most current EC Supply List, for free, and make it easy on yourself to gear up for the journey! (You can also easily download a copy of this from the Book Owners' Website.)

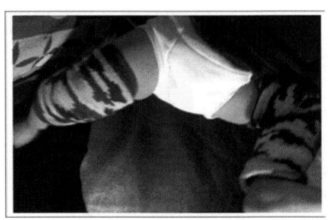

goodbye onesies...hello whitey-tighties & leg-warmers!

As a preview to what you'll see when you download the full list, I've listed the general items below. Most importantly, and at the least, I recommend the following:

- top hat potty & cozy
- mini potty & cozy
- toilet seat reducer

336

- portable potty seat
- prefolds
- cloth diaper covers
- natural disposable diapers
- training pants
- tiny underwear
- elastic-topped pants
- baby t-shirts
- wipes

In addition to the above, some optional but helpful items include:

- long socks
- leg-warmers
- split-crotch pants
- chaps
- diaper belt
- pads
- creams
- wipes warmer
- baby carriers
- carseat protector
- towels & yoga mats
- Post-It sticky notes

Now, go download the full Supply List at godiaperfree.com/supplylist or on the Book Owners' Website and, in it, I'll go through each of the above and share my favorites out of all the categories, plus exactly where you can get them.

APPENDIX 2:
BOOK OWNERS' WEBSITE AND
PRIVATE SUPPORT GROUP

Where can you get access to our Private Support Group, a large private video library, even more support, dozens more answers to questions, and a lots of visual downloads and forms?

Glad you asked!

Sign up for instantaneous access to our Book Owners' Website, a wonderful Members' Area chock-full of further audio-visual EC resources. Again, EC is best learned hands-on, and this is the only multimedia resource that will help you get started, figure out the next step, and complete the process.

**Go to godiaperfree.com/upgrade
to gain access today.**

Our special private website includes a ton of extra support resources including:

- The Private Support Group (including help from me, over 100 Certified Go Diaper Free Coaches, and a worldwide network of parents who've also read this book)
- Troubleshooting Knowledge Base (with additional questions answered and more being added)
- Private Video Library (20+ videos and more being added)
- Downloads Library (dozens of useful forms and logs)
- Special members'-only coupons to WAHM-run EC stores
- Access to Private Consultation (via Skype or telephone)
- And more added periodically.

APPENDIX 3: RESOURCES

Anyone doing EC in a Western country will benefit greatly from support and ideas from others who engage in the same practice. In the physical absence of intact culture & passed-down tradition, ECers have built many niche communities throughout the world, locally and on the Internet.

As your journey will vary from others', and also from time to time, ongoing support and connection in some form is essential to EC (as with many things regarding parenting). Here are two resources offered by Go Diaper Free that should help you find that community.

THE GO DIAPER FREE PRIVATE SUPPORT GROUP

If you have EC questions, **upon** reading this book in its entirety, simply gain access to our Private Support Group here - godiaperfree.com/upgrade - and post away!

Remember, **don't create problems where there are none.** If you go over now and read the posts from the group, you might think everything's gonna go wrong with you, too. But, know that the group only represents about 5% of my total readers. However, don't let this prevent you from posting IF you have a need for support...**please come by!!** That's what it's there for.

Being in a group that is dedicated to parents who've all read the same book will help you stay focused, less distracted, and more supported in the long run.

THE GO DIAPER FREE PODCAST

The Go Diaper Free Podcast is the first of its kind: an audio show that teaches, entertains, and shares about the topic of Elimination Communication. I'm your host and I hope you enjoy the 100+ episodes I've got planned for the coming months and years. If you have something you'd like to hear on the show, email me at andrea@godiaperfree.com. The response so far has been overwhelmingly positive...and the idea of EC is spreading across the airwaves. Subscribe on iTunes to receive notices about new episodes and leave a review while you're there to help increase our reach. All of this is located at godiaperfree.com/iTunes, or simply search iTunes for the podcast, by title above.

And remember...your biggest resources when doing EC are your own HEART and your own GUT instinct. Good luck!

APPENDIX 4:
MORE FROM THE AUTHOR

THE TINY POTTY TRAINING BOOK: A SIMPLE GUIDE FOR NON-COERCIVE POTTY TRAINING

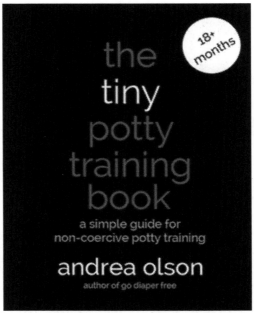

Find it at godiaperfree.com/potty-training-book.

Available in digital and paperback formats, The Tiny Potty Training Book is Andrea's compilation of all the potty training wisdom of today's day and age, minus the fluff, misinformation, and stuff that simply does not work. Non-coercive in its nature, this book will help you wrap up EC with a solid potty training experience and can also help you *finally* train that older child (ages 18 months and up).

Tiny Potty: A teaching book for ages 6 months and up

Find it at godiaperfree.com/tinypotty.

This board book is age and gender neutral. It doesn't mention waiting for "readiness" or the idea of diapers at all. Tiny Potty simply goes through the actual steps of using the toilet in a cute rhyme that teaches the routine to young babies and toddlers in a direct manner. From the self-awareness that baby needs to go, to the final act of washing and drying hands, this book will serve as a fun guide for your baby in the EC or potty learning process, at any age.

APPENDIX 5:
REFERENCES

The following are the books, webpages, persons, and concepts that provided me with ideas & concepts and also served as references, inspiration, and reminders during the creation of this book. With gratitude.

Infant Potty Training: A Gentle and Primeval Method Adapted to Modern Living by Laurie Boucke (2008)

The Diaper-Free Baby: The Natural Toilet Training Alternative by Christine Gross-Loh (2007)

The Attachment Parenting Book: A Commonsense Guide to Understanding and Nurturing Your Baby by Dr. Sears (2001)

The Continuum Concept: In Search of Happiness Lost by Jean Liedloff (1986, 1975)

Parenting From Your Heart: Sharing the Gifts of Compassion, Connection, and Choice by Inbal Kashtan (2004)

Oh Crap! Potty Training by Jamie Glowacki (2012)

BabyCenter.com

Pediatrics Magazine

Wikipedia.org

WebMD.com

Continuum-Concept.org - articles by various authors, including Jean Liedloff

DiaperFreeBaby.org - website, brochures, and select, anonymous members

Indirectly, the Yahoo! Groups I've mentioned in the Resources section of this book have provided inspiration & many reminders.

Kerste Connor, long-time DiaperFreeBaby Mentor in Seattle, WA

EC Simplified: Infant Potty Training Made Easy (no longer available) by Andrea Olson (2011)

Go Diaper Free: A Simple Guide for Elimination Communication, versions 1-4 (no longer available) by Andrea Olson (2013-2015)

ABOUT THE AUTHOR

Andrea Olson, M.A., earned her Master's degree in Psychology from Pacifica Graduate Institute in Carpinteria, California, in 2007. She earned her certificate in movement-based expressive arts therapy in 2007 and, previously, her Bachelor's degree in Business (Entrepreneurship & Strategic Management) in 2000.

Andrea has a knack for taking life's more complicated topics and whittling them down into an accessible, simple form. The result of this is GoDiaperFree.com where she has become a pioneer in helping mothers and fathers worldwide regain their "potty wisdom" with any age child or baby, through both of her books.

Prior to her first pregnancy in 2009, she found that a friend's new baby didn't use diapers. Instead the baby peed into the sink. Intrigued (and living in California where everything weird resides), she decided to practice infant potty training with her future baby from birth. Upon doing EC (elimination communication) with her newborn, she found that it was difficult to translate the EC text into actual practice, so she began writing her first book when her son was

5 months old. When he turned 1, her book became available to the masses via her website, EC Simplified, as a DiaperFreeBaby Mentor in San Francisco, California.

Since that time she's worked with 1,000s of parents worldwide helping them start, maintain, troubleshoot, and graduate EC with babies age 0-18 months. She's since created Go Diaper Free, which is a comprehensive community resource for anyone wanting to stop depending on diapers.

Through her hands-on work with the Go Diaper Free community, she's developed cutting edge work in the infant potty training field and has solved all types of EC challenges, making it easier than ever for parents to free themselves from diaper dependence. This 5th Anniversary Edition of her work brings everything back to its "simplified" roots, and includes everything learned along the way.

She now offers her exclusive, and affordable, line of tiny baby underwear at TinyUndies.com, for babies and toddlers age 6 months to 5T (and sometimes older, if the bottom is tiny enough). She's also written and published a board book for babies 6 months and up, Tiny Potty, and a non-coercive potty training book, The Tiny Potty Training Book, for parents of toddlers 18 months and up (also great for EC completion). It is also Andrea's pleasure to teach coaches worldwide to share the message of EC and potty training in her Go Diaper Free Certified Coach Program.

Andrea lives on a vertitable mini-homestead with her husband, three young children (and one on the way), nanny goat, puppy, kittens, and backyard chickens in lovely Asheville, North Carolina.

Made in the USA
Columbia, SC
04 November 2019